Understanding Employee Stock Options, Rule 144 & Concentrated Stock Position Strategies

Understanding Employee Stock Options, Rule 144 & Concentrated Stock Position Strategies

Travis L. Knapp & Nathan L. Reneau

Writers Club Press
San Jose New York Lincoln Shanghai

Understanding Employee Stock Options, Rule 144 & Concentrated
Stock Position Strategies

Writers Club Press
an imprint of iUniverse.com, Inc.

For information address:
iUniverse.com, Inc.
5220 S 16th, Ste. 200
Lincoln, NE 68512
www.iuniverse.com

ISBN: 0-595-16925-2

Printed in the United States of America

Contents

Foreword

In the late 1990s, I was fortunate enough to participate in the great Internet stock boom, as an employee and option holder in a high-flying Internet technology company. In the past several years, stock options have become a significant portion of many employees' total compensation, where they once were the privilege of company executives, officers, and directors. For me, navigating the process of receiving, exercising, and managing the wealth generated by those stock options has been no simple task.

First, I had to learn about the basics of stock options. This included the basics, like the types of options (Incentive vs. Non-qualified), the relative merits of each, and the standard terms and conditions. Furthermore, I had to learn about buyback provisions, reverse vesting, and other complex concepts that played a large role in determining my ultimate financial situation.

Next, as the company completed its Initial Public Offering, I learned firsthand about lockup periods, blackout periods, structured sales and hedging strategies (which would have been illegal in my case), and other details of managing stock options once there is an actual market for the stock. As I exercised the options, I had to ensure that I paid the proper amount of tax at the time of exercise to avoid nasty penalties at tax time, and so on.

But that just deals with the tactics of managing stock options. On a more strategic level, I had to consider my stock options as a piece of my overall financial situation and portfolio. I had to evaluate how much risk I was taking by holding onto all of my options, how they fit into my overall financial goals, and how I could best use them to achieve those goals with the least risk. These decisions were difficult to make, highly emotionally charged, and had far-reaching implications for my long-term financial situation.

In my case, I spent many hours researching both the tactical and strategic issues. This included calling on friends, professional colleagues, our company's CFO, corporate counsel, and collegiate-level corporate finance and options strategies texts. What I couldn't find was a single book that covered the major issues related to options concepts, concentrated stock positions, tax implications, and diversification strategies.

You are now holding that book.

In my case, it took countless evening hours of research to both learn and understand the concepts contained herein, and they are not to be taken lightly. Many of my co-workers spent less time learning these concepts than they might spend researching what type of car or DVD player to buy. As a result, they watched tens of thousands, hundreds of thousands, or even millions of dollars evaporate—not just "on paper"—but in actual value they could have realized had they made sound strategic decisions in managing their newfound wealth.

In fact, the value of the time you invest understanding and applying the concepts in this book is probably in the thousands of dollars per hour range.

Finally, it is important to note that books like this one are a good starting point for understanding how to grow and remain wealthy via your stock options. But, they are exactly that—a starting point. This book is definitely not a substitute for qualified professional investment, tax, or estate planning advice, since markets, securities and tax laws are constantly subject to change. What this book will give you is the vocabulary and understanding required to evaluate the professional services of those who can help you remain wealthy once you have become wealthy via your stock options.

Scott Miller
Chief Technology Officer
allmystuff, Inc.

PART I

Introduction to Stock Options

Chapter 1

Introduction

The Lure of Options

In the 1800's, millions of risk takers rushed to California with hopes and dreams of finding gold and getting rich. Today, instead of gold, people chase after stock options to fulfill those dreams of becoming wealthy. Many have—by mere luck, hard work or innovation—hit a gold mine and become overnight millionaires; others have not been so fortunate. The interest and demand, by employees for options, have increased the number of companies who offer stock option plans, to more than three thousand. With more than $200 billion, and seven million participants, stock option plans are a major portion of U.S. corporate equity.

However, few of you will ever understand the complex nature of your options, and you may end up making ill-advised and very costly mistakes when exercising and purchasing the underlying stock. Haphazard planning, sometimes based on fear or greed, may cost you thousands and sometimes millions of dollars in unnecessary taxes. After exercising your options, many of you may find most of your net worth concentrated in that stock position. You will then be faced with the complex and difficult task of managing this *concentrated stock position.*

Dealing with options is not an activity for amateurs. Even for many legal, accounting and investment professionals, options can be confusing. This is one area of personal finance where the advice of an expert is invaluable. Anyone presented with the exercising of company options should start with clear financial goals and objectives. If *you* are one of these business professionals, begin by asking yourself the following questions. At the very least, you will be educating yourself to select the right advisor, to work effectively in partnership, and to develop a personalized stock option strategy appropriate for your level of risk-taking and future needs.

- What are my long-term goals?
- When do I want to retire?
- How much after-tax income will I need in retirement?
- What big-ticket purchases do I want to make and how much will they cost? (e.g., house, car)
- Do I hold incentive or nonqualified stock options?
- Will the alternative minimum tax apply to me?
- How should I time the exercise of my options to minimize my tax liability?
- What should I expect to pay in taxes?
- How can I pay for the underlying stock and the taxes, and still hold the stock long enough to benefit from the preferred capital gains tax rate?
- What is the future outlook of the company's stock?

- How will I feel and how will my financial security be affected, if the value of the stock drops dramatically?
- Are there ways to hedge my downside while holding a concentrated position?
- How much of my estate will go to the people I care about?
- What type of estate planning should I pursue before, at, or after exercise?
- What is my overall financial condition, and how do all the different pieces fit together?

The Name of the Game is GROWTH

Stock options have long been a staple of senior executives' compensation packages, but in many cases, options are now being offered to a majority of a company's employees. Employees holding stock options are financially motivated to build and expand the company because the options become valuable only if the price of the company stock goes up. Thus, stock options are considered an implementation of *"pay for performance."*

> Today, information, intellectual property, and human talent are the true building blocks of a company. Businesses use extended vesting schedules as a retention tool, to encourage employees to stay with the company for the longer tenures important in building a cohesive team and the value of the company.

The name of the option game is **growth**. The faster the company grows, the faster the price of its stock rises, and the greater the wealth creation becomes for the shareholders and employees. Everyone—shareholders and employees alike—is on the same side of the table.

The increased use of options has been driven by several factors.

- Founders of many new companies have a management philosophy that employees are ethically entitled to share in the wealth created by their efforts. Historically, key management and senior officers were considered the primary elements of a company's success and, therefore, the only ones entitled to participate in the benefits of a rising stock value.

- Many new and small companies cannot compete with the cash salaries and bonuses paid by the large, established corporations. Therefore, small companies use stock options as a strategy when competing for talent.

- Today, information, intellectual property, and human talent are the true building blocks of a company. Businesses use extended vesting schedules as a retention tool, to encourage employees to stay with the company for the longer tenures important in building a cohesive team and the value of the company.

- Employees, particularly specialists within high tech companies, already face the demands and risks traditionally associated with equity ownership, and, accordingly, are demanding a share of the wealth they create.

For these reasons, stock options, in all of their forms and variations, have become one of the hottest topics in lunchrooms, at company picnics, and within the corporate social structure. They are also one of the single most important elements of many employees' financial security and future.

Finally, company founders and employees—like you—frequently find all of their financial resources and net worth invested in a single company's stock…the very company that will pay their monthly salary to support their family. The risks associated, with such a concentration of resources and dependence on a single source, are enormous, under the best of circumstances. Personal decisions, investment choices, income tax strategies, and estate planning issues are critical to both the founders and employees.

Key Concepts

Astute businessmen have found themselves on the losing side of the equation, because they oversimplified the process. If you are dealing with a great deal of money, you must be educated on the basics of options and seek professional guidance to avoid costly mistakes.

> Stock options can be very confusing and underestimating their complex nature can be costly.

This book is intended to educate you as an investor, to introduce you to the language of stock options, and to inform you on key issues important to personal financial planning and decisions. It provides you with a basic framework, within which you can begin to manage your finances and work towards achieving your personal financial goals.

The key concepts of the stock option experience discussed in this book include the following:

1. The common types of stock option plans and terminology.

2. The basic alternatives and procedures for exercising your options.

3. Certain restrictions and special rules governing the purchase and sale of controlling shareholders', officers', directors' and employees' stock.

4. The basic rules governing the income tax imposed on you, in connection with the exercise of your stock options and the eventual sale of your stock.

5. Some of the basic estate tax rules and issues specifically applicable to stock options and concentrated stock positions.

6. The importance of setting personal goals consistent with your values, as a foundation for designing an overall investment strategy.

7. A simplified explanation of tax and financial strategies, for harnessing the full potential of your stock options and concentrated positions.

Basic Stock Option Concepts

Stock options are intended to give you a participation in future appreciation of the company stock, as measured by the price per share.

Typically, you are given the right to purchase a fixed number of shares (upon vesting), at a price equal to the fair market value of the stock, on the date of grant. If your company has publicly traded stock, it will use the average of the highest and lowest price of the stock traded on that day. The Board of Directors of a closely held company whose shares are *not* traded on an exchange, estimates the fair market value based on advice from experts, such as its chief financial officer, auditors, or consultants specializing in estimating the value of a company's stock. Your right to purchase your company's stock is exercisable in stages—provided you remain a director or employee of the company until the vesting date—and, eventually, expires, after a number of years, typically seven to ten years.

Because the grant of a stock option does not require a monetary investment from you, the option gives you the benefit of all future appreciation during the term of the option, without imposing financial risks of price declines or complete failure of the business. However, you may incur opportunity costs, by accepting a reduced salary or other benefits in exchange for the grant of options.

Laws Governing Stock Options

The granting and exercise of stock options is subject to the securities laws established by the United States Congress. These laws are administered by the Securities and Exchange Commission (SEC). In addition, stock options are also subject to the statutes of states having jurisdiction over the company and the individuals involved in a particular transaction. Federal securities laws and state blue sky laws prohibit certain types of transactions. The most important of these federal statutes and regulations are discussed later. Most state requirements are met once a company fulfills its obligations to have its stock publicly traded, and complies with the federal statutes governing individual transactions.

The profits from your stock options are subject to federal income tax laws, administered by the Internal Revenue Service (IRS), and to state income tax laws, administered by a designated state agency.

The gratuitous transfer of stock or the proceeds from the sale of stock, to a family member through gift or bequest, is taxed under the federal and state gift, estate, and inheritance tax laws.

Understanding the Basic Process and Terms

It is important for you to thoroughly examine the stock option agreement of your company, so that you fully understand the implications of its provisions. The information within the agreement explains your rights as an optionee and the details of the contract. Knowing and understanding these details can help you capture the maximum monetary benefit of the options.

Your company's shareholders adopt a stock option plan to establish a set of rules for granting you stock options. The plan sets rules for determining the price at which the options are granted, when the options can be exercised, when the options expire, and all of the other important terms and provisions of the options granted. Except for the number of shares covered by the option grant, you will be treated the same as every other individual receiving options under that specific plan; however, your company may have more than one plan.

Companies with multiple plans most commonly have an Incentive Stock Option Plan (ISO) and a Nonqualified Stock Option Plan (NSO). The terms of these two different types of plans *will* differ from one another, and senior executive officers frequently participate in both plans, because of the $100,000 per year limitation on options that can be granted to a person as an ISO.

The Board of Directors—or the officers of your company, acting under authority delegated to them by the Board of Directors—determines the number of shares you will be given the right to purchase. Your option to purchase company shares is documented with a written stock option agreement which, at a minimum:

- Sets out the date on which the agreement is effective
- The name of your company
- Your name
- The number of shares that you are given the option to purchase, and
- An agreement by you to comply with certain laws and the terms of the stock option plan

These agreements are prepared by your company's attorneys and tailored to your company's specific circumstances.

It is important for you to thoroughly examine the stock option agreement of your company, so that you fully understand the implications of its provisions. The information within the agreement explains your rights as an optionee and the details of the contract. Knowing and understanding these details can help you capture the maximum monetary benefit of the options.

It is important to note that some provisions may be negotiated between the employee and the company. *(See the Appendix I, for an example of a stock option agreement.)*

Grant. The *grant date* is the date on which the decision is made, as to the number of shares you may purchase. Generally, this is also the date of the stock option agreement between the company and you. In other words, the grant date is the date you are given the option to purchase a specific number of shares at a specific price. This date is important for determining the purchase price for Incentive Stock Options (ISO's) and how long they must be held, pursuant to the option, in order to get favorable long-term capital gains treatment for federal income tax purposes.

> **Example:** On June 15, 2000, Jane, an employee at New Design Semiconductor, is given the option to purchase 60,000 shares of NDS for $5 per share. Her grant date is June 15, 2000, the day she received her options (the date set at the board meeting.)

Exercise. You have exercised your option, when you pay the exercise price to your company and the company delivers the stock to you (you purchase your company's stock). The *exercise date* is the date on which you notify your company of your irrevocable decision to exercise a specific number your options. The final settlement of the transaction may be several days or weeks later, depending upon the circumstances. The *exercise price* or *strike price* is the price that you pay when you exercise the option and purchase the stock.

> **Example:** When Jane elects to exercise her options, her exercise price or cost is $5 per share. This is the price she pays for her shares, even if the stock is selling for $20, on the exercise date.

Vesting. Your stock option is fully vested, when you are entitled to exercise the option to purchase your company stock and to dispose of it in any manner you determine, without any further restrictions from your company. Historically, stock options have become vested and exercisable on the same dates; however, increasingly, current plans are now permitting recipients to exercise their options before they have a fully vested right to sell or transfer the company stock. (See sections on reverse vesting and Section 83(b).)

A typical agreement in which the options are both vested and exercisable on the same date might be as follows:

Example: On June 15, 2000, Jane, the Vice-president of Manufacturing for New Design Semiconductor, is given the right to purchase stock of the company, according to the following schedule:

Example of Vesting Schedule

No. of Shares	Exercise Price per Share	Date on which Vested and First Exercisable	Date on which Option Expires
15,000	$5.00	June 15, 2001	June 15, 2010
15,000	$5.00	June 15, 2002	June 15, 2010
15,000	$5.00	June 15, 2003	June 15, 2010
15,000	$5.00	June 15, 2004	June 15, 2010
60,000			

Figure 1.1

Jane can purchase the first 15,000 shares at any time, between June 15, 2001 and June 15, 2010, for $5 per share. Immediately upon exercise, she can sell or transfer the stock, without restriction by the company; however, she may be subject to other restrictions under the federal securities laws (See Chapter 4).

The following is a visual example of a yearly vesting schedule (though options may also vest monthly, or quarterly).

Visual of Annual Vesting Schedule

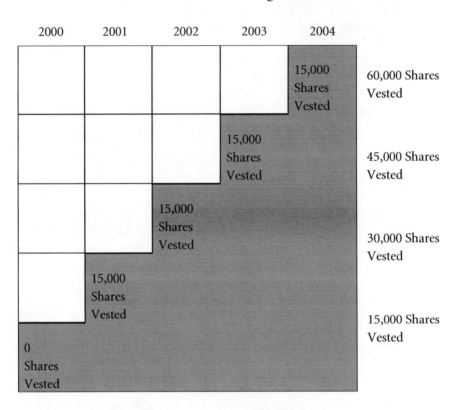

Figure 1.2

Occasionally, a company may use a *cliff* vesting schedule in which all the covered options vest on a particular date.

Example: A key employee is given the option to purchase 60,000 shares for $5 per share, and all of the options are fully vested on the first anniversary of her hire date.

Holding period. The holding period is a tax term that refers to the time between the date on which you exercise the option to purchase company stock and the date on which you make a disposition of the company stock.

> **Example:** If Jane exercises her option, to purchase the first 15,000 shares on June 15, 2001, but does not sell the stock until November 15, 2002, she has a holding period of 17 months. The difference between the market value, on the date of exercise, and the subsequent sales price will be taxed, as either a long-term capital gain or long-term capital loss.

Disposition. A disposition (getting rid of the stock) is the transfer of company stock by sale, gift or otherwise. Timing is important for determining the tax consequences of a disposition.

Expiration date. The expiration date is the last date on which you may purchase stock, under the terms of the stock option agreement with your company. Stock option plans usually provide that options granted to you will expire on a date that is a fixed period (usually seven to ten years) from the grant date. Your company may have a very short grace period, but we don't suggest testing the boundaries. Also, your options generally will expire 30 to 90 days after either your death or termination of employment.

> **Example:** All of Jane's options expire on June 15, 2010, ten years after the options were originally granted.

This is a very important date, because you will lose all your unrealized profits, if your option to purchase the shares expires unexercised. For example, we had a client who waited until the literal expiration date to exercise her Dell stock, which had a bargain element of more than one million dollars. Since the process involved a coordination of parties and the preparation of legal documents, you can imagine the stress during the transaction, with a million dollars at risk. *Always plan ahead for the exercise of your options.*

Bargain element. The bargain element is the difference between the fair market value of the underlying stock and the exercise price of the option.

> **Example:** If Jane has 15,000 options of New Design Semiconductors that have a current share price of $20, and her exercise price is $5, her bargain element is $15 per share.

Note: Do not confuse the bargain element with *net benefit*. Net benefit, or net investible dollars, is the sum left over, after subtracting the taxes and the transaction costs from the bargain element.

Underwater. If your stock's market price is less than your exercise price, the stock is said to be underwater. In this case, it makes no sense to exercise the options. They are worthless. If you are still optimistic about the future of your company, you may purchase the stock on the open market or simply hold the option, until it becomes profitable.

> If your stock's market price is less than your exercise price, the stock is said to be underwater. In this case, it makes no sense to exercise the options.

Re-price. Companies will seldom re-price, or lower the options exercise price to market value, even if they remain under water. Re-pricing may cause shareholders to lose confidence in the stock. If the company chooses to re-price, it will normally also extend the vesting date. Instead of re-pricing options, a company will normally grant new options with a lower exercise price.

Other Provisions

Each company may structure a stock option agreement with different provisions. A typical plan may include a variety of the following. *(See an example of a Stock Option Agreement in the Appendix I.)*

Change of control. Currently, the change of control provision is a hot topic within the high tech community. The change of control provision describes the vesting, exercise, dilution, and similar issues, which become critical when there is an acquisition or merger.

Non-transferability. A non-transferability provision may indicate that the option may not be transferred for any reason (e.g., assignment, transfer to another person or entity, mortgage, or pledge), except upon your death. In other words, you are the only one who can exercise the options during your lifetime.

Termination of employment. The termination of employment provision explains the general determinations made by your company's Board about the fate of your options, upon termination of your employment. In some cases, the Board of Directors may reserve the right to review the matter and make case-by-case decisions, depending on whether the termination was for *cause* (you failed to properly perform your duties or any other justifiable reason) or *not cause*. Other agreements may specify an amount of time after termination, such as three months, for you to exercise your options. Later, we will discuss the risk of being terminated and losing all rights to your options.

> If you are holding exercisable options with large bargain elements, do not wait to review your stock option agreement, so that you will understand exactly what you have at risk.

Death and disability provision. The death and disability of optionee provision explains the terms in which your options may be transferred, if you die or become disabled. The transfer is normally subject to your last will and can be made within one year, but not after ten years.

Anti-dilution provision. An anti-dilution provision ensures that the value of your options will not be diluted by reason of stock dividends, recapitalizations, mergers, consolidations, split-ups, exchanges of shares, or any other type of transaction. Most anti-dilution provisions use formulas and value comparisons to adjust the number of option shares, to give you equitable treatment. For example, most anti-dilution provisions will automatically double the number of option shares, when the company implements a 2 for 1 stock split.

Anti-dilution provisions usually do not prevent a reduction of ownership percentages when additional capital is contributed to the company, especially new companies.

Reload provision. A reload provision enables you to maximize the potential of your options. If you decide to participate in this transaction, the options will reload (the company will issue new stock options), when the option stock is paid for with company stock. New options are issued, in the same amount as the number of shares used to pay the exercise price, and have an exercise price equal to share price on the exercise date. The expiration date will remain the same as the original options. The reload provision allows you to capture incremental appreciation by exercising and disposing of the stock, while retaining participation in future appreciation through the reload options. Tax considerations are very complicated, and require the attention of a tax professional.

Chapter 2

Types of Stock Options and Compensation Plans

Basic Types of Stock Options and Their Equivalents

Companies use different types of stock option plans to attract, retain, and reward employees, and knowing the type of stock options you have is very important. The two main types are Incentive Stock Options (ISO's) and Nonqualified Stock Options (NSO's); Incentive Stock Options generally are considered more desirable. Only company employees can hold Incentive Stock Options. Both employees and non-employees, such as consultants, can hold Nonqualified Options. Employees, particularly senior officers, may hold both Incentive Stock Options and Nonqualified Stock Options. You need a specific strategy for each type of option, if you hold both. Your stock option agreement will usually tell you the type of option granted.

Congress has endorsed the concept of using compensatory stock options, by providing for preferential tax treatments. The main difference between ISO's and NSO's is the way they are taxed. ISO's have a substantial tax advantage over NSO's, and it is important to understand the differences. The rules dictate when income is recognized and when you will be responsible for paying the taxes on the bargain element.

Other Equity Compensation

Companies also use Employee Stock Purchase Plans (ESPP) to encourage stock ownership and to accomplish their goals. ESPP's are similar to ISO's and have certain holding periods and rules, to qualify for long-term capital gains tax.

A related strategy, often called reverse vesting or "early exercise", is when your company sells you stock (at either fair market price or at a bargain) that is subject to restrictions, which require you to resell the stock to your employer, if you voluntarily or involuntarily terminate your relationship with the company. The restrictions in the repurchase agreement can defer the tax consequences relating to the bargain element, if any, at the time of the conditional sale. You may have an opportunity to make an election to pay tax on the bargain element on the date of purchase, rather than when the resale obligation expires. Later in this book, we will discuss reverse vesting and the related *"Section 83(b) election"* in detail.

Incentive Stock Options

Incentive Stock Options (frequently referred to as "ISO's" or "Statutory Stock Options") permit your employer to grant purchase options to you, and other company employees, without any immediate tax consequences. In general, you are allowed to exercise the options to purchase stock at a bargain price, with limited or no immediate income tax consequences. *See Alternative Minimum Tax* later in this chapter.

> In general, you are allowed to exercise the options to purchase stock at a bargain price, with limited or no immediate income tax consequences.

Required Provisions

Briefly, an incentive stock option must fit the following rules in order for you to get the favorable tax treatment provided by Congress:

1. The option must be granted to an employee of the company or a subsidiary.
2. The exercise price must be equal to the fair market price of the stock on the date of grant.
3. The exercise price must be 110% of the fair market value of the stock if the optionee owns 10% or more of the company stock.
4. The option must have been issued pursuant to a written option plan approved by the shareholders of the company.
5. There has to be a written option agreement between the company and the employee.
6. All options have to expire no later than ten years after the grant date.
7. The option agreement must specifically state that the options cannot be transferred, other than by death, and cannot be exercised by anyone, other than the optionee.
8. The number of options granted to any one individual is limited. The aggregate exercise price of options first exercisable in any one year may not exceed $100,000.

These technical details can confuse even lawyers and CPA's who do not specialize in employee compensation plans. As the recipient of options, you only need to know that the company has hired tax experts to design an Incentive Stock Option Plan, that your agreement with your company designates your options as Incentive Stock Options, and that the maximum aggregate cost of options first exercisable, in any one year, is less than $100,000. When option grants exceed the $100,000 limitation, the excess becomes Nonqualified Stock Options (discussed in the next section). The rules for determining which specific options are Incentive Stock Options and which are Nonqualified Stock Options are extremely important. The proper segregation is critical when the exercise prices of several different grants vary and when you elect to make partial exercises. The rules are both ambiguous and complex, so the assistance of knowledgeable tax experts is essential.

Income Tax Rules

The unique perk in ISO's is the preferential tax treatment allowed by the federal income tax laws. In general, the grant of the option does not cause you to have a tax liability and the exercise does not create any regular income tax liability, as long as you do not make a *disqualifying disposition.*

A *disqualifying disposition* is the transfer of the stock less than two years after the original grant of the option, or less than one year after the exercise of the option; in which case, you will not benefit from the capital gains tax rate, but will be subject to the ordinary income tax rates. This includes virtually every type of transfer by sale, exchange, gift or transfer of legal title, except for transfer by death, transfers in certain tax-free corporate reorganizations, certain transactions between spouses, and certain bankruptcy transactions. This particular restriction makes estate planning especially difficult.

> A *disqualifying disposition* is the transfer of the stock less than two years after the original grant of the option, or less than one year after the exercise of the option; in which case, you will not benefit from the capital gains tax rate, but will be subject to the ordinary income tax rates.

The difference between the exercise price and the sale price of stock sold after the required two-year and one-year holding periods is taxed at the long-term capital gains rates, currently a maximum of twenty percent. By contrast, the profits from disqualifying dispositions are classified as compensation income and taxed as part of your ordinary income, in many cases, nearly twice the capital gains rate. While the tax laws are not especially clear on the subject, the Internal Revenue Service currently interprets them, to allow your employer to forego the withholding of either regular income taxes or the employment taxes for Social Security old age benefits and Medicare.

If you are holding incentive stock options you need to explore making a *Section 83(b) election,* discussed in detail later in the chapter, under the nonqualified section.

Alternative Minimum Tax (AMT)

Now comes the iron fist inside the silk glove. The difference between the exercise price and the fair market value on the date of exercise is considered income, for purposes of the alternative minimum tax (AMT). This becomes a major issue when a substantial number of ISO's are exercised in a calendar year.

The Alternative Minimum Tax, technically applicable to every taxpayer, was originally created to limit the number of loopholes used by the wealthy, and to require them to pay their fair share of federal taxes. Every taxpayer is required to pay the greater of the tax, computed the regular way, and the tax, computed using the AMT computation. Because the purpose of the AMT is to reach high-income taxpayers, who benefit from the preferential provisions of the tax law, few lower and middle-income taxpayers are aware of the computation. In fact, the form for computing the liability (Form 6251) does not need to be attached to a return unless the tax applies.

> The Alternative Minimum Tax, technically applicable to every tax-payer, was originally created to limit the number of loopholes used by the wealthy, and to require them to pay their fair share of federal taxes. Every taxpayer is required to pay the greater of the tax, computed the regular way, and the tax, computed using the AMT computation.

Mechanically, the alternative minimum tax shows up as an incremental addition to a taxpayer's overall liability.

Example: Jane has a regular tax liability of $125,000, net of all credits, that appears on line 49 of her 1999 Form 1040. The alternative minimum tax computation, on Form 6251, shows a total liability of $130,000 (called the tentative alternative minimum tax). The difference between the tentative AMT and the regular tax, $5,000, is entered on line 51, of Jane's return. The total tax Jane is required to pay is $130,000, the amount of the tentative alternative minimum tax.

The alternative minimum tax is computed by adjusting regular taxable income for certain income and deductions that receive preferential treatment for regular income tax purposes. Common adjustments include the unrealized gain on Incentive Stock Options, personal exemptions, the standard deduction, interest on second mortgages, medical expenses, miscellaneous itemized deductions, exempt interest on certain municipal bonds, and a host of special business and tax shelter items. Under current tax law (year 2000), an exclusion of $33,750 for single individuals and $45,000, for married couples, is available to reduce the alternative minimum tax; however, the exclusion is phased out for single individuals having alternative minimum taxable income of $112,500 to $247,500, and for married couples having alternative minimum taxable income of $150,000 to $330,000. The resulting alternative minimum taxable income is taxed at a rate of 26% to 28%. (*A copy of the 1999 Form 6251, which includes information on the items of adjustment, the phase-out of the exclusion, and the tax rates for single and married taxpayers, is in the Appendix IV.*)

Congress classified some of the AMT adjustments as "timing adjustments," because the primary benefit, of the preferential treatment accorded those items, was to materially delay the tax liability associated with the income or expenditure. Congress treats the unrealized ISO appreciation, included in the alternative minimum taxable income, as a timing adjustment. Congress further provided that the AMT associated with timing adjustments may be recovered as a credit against the regular tax in future years.

The theory of imposing a "temporary" tax, on the excessive benefit from timing adjustments, has a great logical appeal; however, as with many tax concepts, it breaks down in practical application.

First, the computations for the initial AMT and the allowance of a credit for recovery in future years are complex and frequently affected by income and deductions other than those related to the exercise of a stock option and the eventual sale of the related security. The tax consequences of exercising stock options and the subsequent sale of the related securities may vary greatly from one employee to another.

Second, the amount of credit available for carry over is recalculated each year. Certain combinations of circumstances can cause the credit to "evaporate" over time. For example, you might pay AMT of $35,000, in the year 2000. You may sell the stock you received in connection with the exercise in the year 2004, and expect to have a significant portion of your capital gains tax to be offset by the AMT credit, only to find that a large portion of the credit no longer exists.

Third, the obvious concern is that the AMT may, under some circumstances, be imposed at a rate of 28%, when the long-term capital gains rate is only 20%. The AMT credit may not completely reverse the effects of this punitive tax rate. The only effective defense against this complex and burdensome tax structure is to prepare pro-forma models of your alternatives for option exercises to determine the potential tax consequences of each one. Frequently, you will find that planning will significantly reduce the tax burden on your options and encourage you to favor one strategy over another.

Summary

Incentive Stock Options are considered tax sheltered compensation provided for under federal income tax law. The options must be non-transferable and issued under a plan approved by the company's shareholders. The plan must conform to statutory limitations on the amount of options you, as an employee, may be given, the exercise price of the options, the duration of the options, and certain other technical limitations. There is no income tax on the grant of the option, but the exercise of the options may require you to pay an alternative minimum tax. The profit from shares sold less than two years after the date of your option agreement with your company (the grant date) or less than one year after you have exercised the options is taxable as ordinary income. The profit, from shares held more than the required two years from grant and one year from exercise date, is taxed as long-term capital gains. The maximum rate on long-term capital gains is 20%.

Employee Stock Purchase Plans

The second equity-based compensatory plan, allowed preferential tax treatment by Congress, is the Employee Stock Purchase Plan (ESPP). Such plans are generally implemented similarly to an employee savings plan. Money is withheld from your regular paycheck and used to purchase company stock at a discounted price, on a regularly scheduled basis.

A common approach is for you to elect to have your company withhold a percentage of your after tax salary. You can elect any amount, up to a maximum set by your company plan. Typically, every six months, the money withheld from your paycheck is used to purchase company stock, at a price equal to 85% of the fair market value of the stock. The method for determining the fair market price is prescribed by the plan and, frequently, is an average over a 6 to 12 month period, or the closing price on a particular date. The reference date for determining the fair market price of the company stock varies from plan to plan. You have no taxable income at the time of the purchase, and if you hold the stock for a qualifying period, you pay only long-term capital gains rates on the profit when the stock is sold.

Basic Rules

The rules for Employee Stock Purchase Plans are found in Section 423 of the Internal Revenue Code, and, hence, may also be called Section 423 Plans. To qualify, a plan must allow participation by all employees, except the following:

- Those employed less than two years
- Employees who customarily work less than 20 hours per week
- Seasonal employees, who usually work five months or less each year
- Certain highly compensated employees

Other general requirements, required for plan participants to receive the favorable tax treatment, are as follows:

- An employee may not purchase more than $25,000 of company stock, for each year the employee has held options under the option grant.
- A person must be employed by the company for at least three months before purchasing stock from a plan.
- An employee must hold the stock for two years from the grant date and twelve months from the exercise date. The definition of a disqualifying disposition is essentially the same for an Employee Stock Purchase Plan and for an ISO.

These plans are designed to require broad coverage that benefits all employees, regardless of position in the company. As generally structured, they encourage long-term savings by the employees and long-term holding of the company stock. However, creative use of the rules can sometimes provide lucrative compensation to employees.

Example: The fair market value of company stock is $5 on September 1, 1999, when a plan is established. You are given the option of investing up to 15% of your salary in the stock, for the next two years, at a fixed price of $5 per share. If the stock price increases to $20 per share by June 2000, and if you earn $100,000 per year and invest 15% of your salary for the first six months of year 2000, you will purchase 1,500 shares of stock for $7,500 [(100,000/2) x 15% = $7,500; $7,500/$5 = 1,500 shares]. This represents equity compensation of $22,500, in addition to your regular salary (1,500 x 20 = $30,000; $30,000—$7,500 = $22,500).

Frequently, you are allowed to hedge your risk. You can elect to have a percentage or fixed amount withheld from each paycheck for six months. At the end of the six months, the money can be used to purchase stock, or if you prefer, the money withheld is returned to you, plus interest, from the date withheld, at a market rate.

Example: You elect to have $1,000 per month withheld from your monthly salary, when the company stock is trading for $100 per share, and you have the option, under your ESPP, to purchase the stock for $85 per share. At the end of six months, your company is holding $6,000 of your money, but the stock is selling for $75 per share. Because the market price is $10 less than your ESPP price, you should elect to take the $6,000, plus interest at current CD rates, rather than purchasing the stock.

Unlike an ISO, there is no adjustment to the alternative minimum taxable income for the bargain element of an ESPP purchase.

Tax Withholding

The bargain element of an ESPP purchase is treated as compensation income when there is a disqualifying disposition. In other words, if you do not fulfill the holding requirements, you will be paying ordinary income tax instead of the preferred capital gains tax. Recent private letter rulings indicate it is the IRS's view that an employer is required to withhold federal income taxes and FICA employment taxes. You should rely upon your employer's tax advisors and comply with company policies in this regard.

Nonqualified Stock Options (NSO's)

Nonqualified Stock Options also permit your employer to grant purchase options, without any immediate tax consequences; however, unlike ISO's, a tax burden is placed on you at the time the options are exercised. Understanding how NSO's work is critical, if you are fortunate enough to work for a company with a Nonqualified Stock Option plan and to be given a share of the options.

> Nonqualified Stock Options also permit your employer to grant purchase options, without any immediate tax consequences; however, unlike ISO's, a tax burden is placed on you at the time the options are exercised.

Basic Rules

Nonqualified Stock Options may be granted to both employees and others (such as consultants and outside attorneys), in amounts or on terms that do not comply with the provisions governing Incentive Stock Options. Generally, the non-compliance is intentional and recognized from inception, by both your employer and you. Like Incentive Stock Options, certain rules prescribe minimum basic terms that must be included in the underlying plan and the agreement between your employer and you. The rules, however, are generally more liberal and allow the parties more flexibility than the rules governing Incentive Stock Options.

There is no income taxable to you and your employer has no deduction at the time of the grant, unless you make a special election to be treated otherwise. The tax due upon exercise of the option is materially different from that due upon exercise of an Incentive Stock Option. You must recognize the entire bargain element of the purchase as taxable income, and your employer gets a matching deduction against its taxable income. Remember, the difference between the fair market value on the date of purchase and the price paid by the employee is the bargain element. This income is considered to be your compensation for services rendered to your company, and your company is required to withhold federal income tax and applicable Social Security/Medicare taxes, subject to the annual limitations. Gain on the subsequent sale of the stock is treated as either short-term capital gain (maximum of 39.6%) or long-term capital gain (maximum 20%), depending upon how much time expires in the interim.

Once you have exercised an NSO, you acquire title to the company stock, but may not have to immediately recognize income and pay taxes. The obligation to pay tax on the bargain element of the purchase depends upon whether you have unrestricted control over the stock and the ability to sell it, without being penalized under the federal securities laws.

In general, Congress decided to tax the compensation associated with Nonqualified Stock Options at the time the options are exercised. You are, therefore, immediately responsible for the taxes on the bargain element. On the surface, the rules are straightforward. Unlike Incentive Stock Options, the exercise price can be anything your company chooses. Again, NSO's are frequently granted to directors, who are not employees, and may be granted to company attorneys, accountants, and other similar independent contractors.

Some companies elect to use only Nonqualified Stock Options for compensatory purposes; however, the typical NSO is a supplement to an Incentive Stock Option plan with the options being granted to directors, who cannot qualify for ISO's. NSO's are also used to make grants, which exceed the Incentive Stock Option limitations of $100,000 in exercise price per year to senior officers and other highly compensated individuals.

The terminology of NSO's is generally the same as for ISO's, and in most cases, the exercise price is near the market value of your company stock on the grant date. Typically, the options are vest over three to five years, and expire seven to ten years from the grant date. Because NSO's are not subject to the rigid rules of ISO's, your company can allow exercise on the grant date. Some start-ups allow founders and senior executives to exercise as much as one-third of their options immediately upon grant. Your company may also benefit you as an option holder by setting the exercise price well below the market value of its stock.

Typically, NSO's are not transferable except upon your death. This is largely a matter of company policy, and some NSO plans allow transfers to your family members or family trust, in order to facilitate various estate planning strategies. NSO's rarely permit the sale of your option contract, or other transfer, to an unrelated party; however, to the extent such a transfer is permitted, you pay tax on the proceeds from the sale and have no further tax liability associated with the option. In those limited situations, where a transfer to a family member or trust is permitted, the stock typically will be transferred to a trust for a child or grandchild. If the transfer of your option is a completed gift, it is subject to the general rules for gratuitous transfers, and a gift tax may be payable to the IRS. On a positive note, the value of the option for computation of gift and estate taxes is frozen as of the date of transfer, but you, the grantor, will be liable for the entire income tax on the bargain element, at the time your trust exercises the option.

Note: This can be used to gain some leverage on the gift tax system, since your payment of the income tax is not considered to be a gift to your trust beneficiary. The impact of an early transfer of an option, when it has limited value, combined with your payment of the income tax, after there is substantial appreciation, can efficiently move a large asset base to the next generation. The obvious caveat is that you, the donor, must be both willing and financially able to pay an income tax of substantial, unknown, and potentially immense amount.

Once you have exercised an NSO, you acquire title to the company stock, but may not have to immediately recognize income and pay taxes. The obligation to pay tax on the bargain element of the purchase depends upon whether you have unrestricted control over the stock and the ability to sell it, without being penalized under the federal securities laws. If there is a substantial risk of forfeiture, due to the federal securities laws, the general rules of Section 83 apply. You will recognize income and pay tax, when the restrictions lapse. The significance, of transfer restrictions and the SEC rules affecting certain officers' sale of stock, is discussed in the next section, which explains the rules of Section 83 in greater detail.

The holding period, for purposes of gaining the benefits of the federal long-term capital gains rate, starts on the date the bargain element of the purchase becomes taxable income, to the employee.

The Role of Section 83: Substantial Risk of Forfeiture and Restrictions on Transfer

Section 83 of the Internal Revenue Code broadly applies to all transfers of property, in connection with the performance of services, generally as compensation. However, it is normally associated with a narrow group of transactions, in which your right to use and enjoy the benefits of the property are restricted, and most importantly, subject to a substantial risk of forfeiture.

The law takes a philosophical approach that as long as you (the service provider) are at risk of losing the economic benefit of the property, it is not good policy to make you pay the tax on the benefit of receiving the property, until you have gained a fully vested interest in the property.

> If you utilize Section 83(b), you elect to recognize income and pay tax on the bargain element immediately upon acquiring stock, rather than waiting until you have fulfilled all the conditions for unrestricted ownership, in which case you will be obligated to resell your shares to your company, if you do not fulfill the vesting requirements.

In general, you (the service provider) do not recognize income, when the property is transferred to you, if the property is restricted and subject to a substantial risk of forfeiture. The classic example of a substantial risk of forfeiture is an agreement that bases full ownership of the property upon the "future performance of substantial services." This sometimes is referred to as an *"earn-out"* restriction. Since there is always a possibility that you may not fulfill your obligation, income from the transfer of the property is not determined and is not taxable to you, until completion of the required service.

Section 16(b), of the Securities and Exchange Act of 1934, creates another risk of forfeiture recognized by Section 83. Section 16(b) requires certain officers and directors to disgorge all profits from stock held less than six months. The rules of Section 16(b) can be exceedingly complex, and the actual Section 16(b) limitation, on the sale of stock acquired by an option exercise, may be anywhere from zero to more than six months. The income tax regulations avoid the complications of examining each shareholder's particular circumstances, by using a strict six-month presumption for everyone. *(Section 16(b) is discussed in greater detail in Chapter 4.)*

Section 83 delays the taxable event, only if the property (the company stock) is subject to both a substantial risk of forfeiture and a restriction on transferability.

Section 83(b) Election

You may make a Section 83(b) election as a tax planning strategy.

You may elect to exercise your options prior to the actual vesting date, and before there is a significant appreciation, in order to minimize the bargain element and reduce the tax liability. If you utilize Section 83(b), you elect to recognize income and pay tax on the bargain element immediately upon acquiring stock, rather than waiting until you have fulfilled all the conditions for ownership, in which case you will be obli-gated to resell your shares to your company, if you do not fulfill the vesting requirements.

> You make a Section 83(b) election, by filing a statement with the Internal Revenue Service within 30 days after you receive the property (shares of restricted stock).

NOTE: Section 83 does not permit this election to be made in connection with the *grant* of most NSO's.

> **Example:** Assume Jane held NSO's rather than ISO's and was permitted to exercise them immediately upon grant, subject to an obligation to resell them, if she quit before the vesting date. She might elect to exercise the options immediately and make a Section 83(b) election. If she made the election on 60,000 shares, when they were trading $5, her exercise price, she would have no tax liability, because the market price and the exercise price would be the same. Her holding period would start immediately, and the profit from selling the stock at $20, after it is fully vested, would be taxed as a long-term capital gains (20%). If she waits to exercise the NSO's, she will pay ordinary income tax rates on the $900,000 bargain element ($15 x 60,000 x 39.6% = $356,400). The long-term capital gains rate from a Section 83(b) election would be only about half ($900,000 x 20% = $180,000). That would be a significant savings of approximately $176,400.

This strategy works best for start-up companies, where a significant part of the option value is the simply privilege of participating in ownership

An emerging trend with ISO plans and NSO plans, of start-up and private companies, is to permit you—the plan participant—to exercise your options early, in the term of the agreement. Frequently, the exercise price is low and you need make only a small investment in order to acquire the stock. You cannot transfer the stock and must agree to resell the stock to the company for the option price, if you leave before ownership is fully vested. Frequently, ownership of the stock vests over a period of years, similar to the exercise rights under the traditional ISO and NSO plans. By holding stock, rather than the options, you qualify to make a Section 83(b) election at a time when there is little or no bargain element. You pay little or no immediate income tax.

If you exercise your options, pay for the stock, and make a Section 83(b) election, you have invested hard cash in the company and are at risk of losing all of your money if the company fails.

For example, if you have an option to purchase a million shares at twenty-five cents, exercising the options will cost $250,000. That's not a small investment. If you do not have the cash to pay for the shares, many times your company will loan you the amount needed to purchase the shares, as a fringe benefit. Brokerage firms and banks rarely loan money for the purchase of stock that is not publicly traded.

A second strategy is to exercise options ahead of an IPO, in order to avoid the tax from the sudden and frequently substantial appreciation associated with the new visibility and marketability of the stock. This strategy allows you to get an early start on your holding period for the stock, and to move as quickly as possible from the high tax rates on ordinary income to the more favorable rates on long-term capital gains. This strategy also serves to reduce or eliminate the alternative minimum tax problem associated with an ISO.

One risk associated with a Section 83(b) election is that you are not allowed a deduction for the bargain element, if the stock becomes worthless, or if it is sold for less than the fair market value on the date of exercise.

> **Example:** If Jane exercises 15,000 of her $5 NSO options on October 30, 2000, when the fair market value is $12 per share and she makes a Section 83(b) election, she will pay tax on $105,000. She will have a total tax basis of $180,000, $75,000 cash paid for the shares plus $105,000 of taxable income (at a cost of approximately $41,580 in taxes if she is in the top bracket). If the company fails, her deduction for the worthless stock is limited to $75,000, the cash purchase price.

Because a resale obligation is a substantial risk of forfeiture, a Section 83(b) election *must be made* in order to get the desired tax benefits. The main point is to turn ordinary income tax (up to 39.6%) into long-term capital gains (20%), as quickly as possible.

Making the Section 83(b) Election

You make a Section 83(b) election, by filing a statement with the Internal Revenue Service within 30 days after you receive the property (shares of restricted stock). The IRS has not created a form on which to make the election, so you must furnish the required information on a plain sheet of paper that is boldly labeled "Section 83(b) Election" at the top. Many companies include a Section 83(b) election form with the option agreement. The election should begin with "The undersigned taxpayer hereby elects under Section 83(b) as follows," followed by these items:

1. Your name and social security number.

2. A description of the stock or other restricted property received as compensation.

3. The date on which you received the property and the taxable year for which the election is made.

4. The nature of the restrictions on the stock.

5. The fair market value of the stock at the time you acquired it. The fair market value may be affected by a lack of marketability, a minority position and the current operating condition of the company; however, the possibility of forfeiture on account of the restrictions relating to the Section 83(b) election may not be taken into consideration when determining the fair market value of the company.

6. The amount you paid for the stock.

7. A statement declaring: "I have provided copies of this statement, as required under the regulations for Section 83."

A copy of the statement must be provided to the company issuing the stock and a copy must be attached to your tax return for the year of the election.

The election is made by mailing the statement to the same IRS office where you are required to file your annual income tax return. Again, the election must be filed within 30 days of receiving the stock, and should be carefully documented, because you will have the burden of proving strict compliance with the rules, if there are ever any questions from the IRS. The election form should be filed by registered mail, return receipt requested. Both the receipt from the deposit of the envelope with the Postal Service and the return receipt should be permanently retained in your records.

Withholding Taxes and FICA

Your employer must withhold taxes (or get a cash reimbursement) from you, if you are exercising an NSO.

These taxes include both the employment taxes (Federal Insurance Contribution Act, Social Security taxes for old age benefits and Medicare) and federal income taxes. In the case of NSO's, taxes are withheld on the exercise date.

The amount of FICA tax due in connection with the exercise of an NSO will depend upon your cumulative earnings prior to the exercise date. If your earnings exceed the annual limitation, with regard to old age benefits, they will be subject only to the Medicare portion of the tax (1.45% for the employee). If your cumulative wages and salary are less than the annual limitation, they will be subject to the full tax rate on all or part of the taxable income attributable to the option exercise. Federal income tax can be withheld at the supplemental rate of 28%, if your employer has been withholding taxes from your regular paychecks.

The difficult issue facing your employer is how to withhold taxes on your wages, if no cash is being transferred to you. Typically, you must pay the taxes before your company will release the stock certificates.

The simple approach is to have you make a direct payment of the taxes to your employer, simultaneous with the delivery of the certificates. An alternative is for your employer to deliver a reduced number of shares and sell the portion withheld, to cover the taxes.

> **Example:** If Jane wants to exercise NSO's for 15,000 shares at $5 per share, she must pay the company $75,000 for the exercise price. Assuming the stock has a market price of $20 per

share, she must also pay the company $66,262.50 for taxes, before the company will release the certificates. Income taxes of $63,000 [($20–$5) x 15,000 x 28%] plus Medicare of $3,262.50 ($225,000 x 1.45%).

As can be expected, this issue alone requires careful planning when the amount of cash needed for taxes is more than your personal savings balance. We examine the strategies for solving this problem in the later sections, along with strategies for maximizing the value of your options.

> Don't be surprised at the end of the year when you figure your taxes, if you still owe the IRS a hefty sum, because the amount of tax on your exercise is more than what was withheld by your employer.

Example: If you have a bargain element of one million dollars, your employer will likely withhold the usual 28% or $280,000. However, if you are in the 39.6% tax bracket, the total tax bill will be $396,000. You will still need to pay an extra $116,000 in taxes.

You are required to pay your taxes as you go through the year, and penalties may apply if you owe more than the amount withheld by your employer. You should always consult a tax advisor immediately when exercising options.

Reverse Vesting (Pre IPO)

We have covered the basics of incentive stock options (ISO's) and non-qualified stock options (NSO's), and how a Section 83(b) election may be used to help save taxes. Now, we will discuss the reverse vesting that is a growing trend among high-tech start-ups. Realizing that Uncle Sam can immediately take up to 39.6% of the bargain element when appreciated options are exercised, many start-ups that do not have publicly traded stock structure plans that allow options to be exercised the day they are granted. The catch to this strategy is that ownership of stock is not fully vested for a specified time, normally one to five years. If you leave the company before ownership is vested, you must resell the shares to the company for the exercise price.

> Reverse vesting allows you to exercise the option when there is little or no bargain element. This means there is little or no alternative minimum tax adjustment for ISO's and little or no ordinary income for NSO's.

Further, the holding period, for avoiding a disqualifying disposition of ISO stock and for obtaining favorable long-term capital gains treatment, starts immediately. Because the resale obligation is a substantial risk of forfeiture, a Section 83(b) election *must be made* in order to get the desired tax benefits. The main point is to turn ordinary income tax (up to 39.6%) into long-term capital gains (20%), as quickly as possible.

Reverse vesting also allows you to purchase shares *after* the grant date, but *before* the company stock dramatically appreciates, as a result of its Initial Public Offering. This allows you to reduce your risk, by waiting until your company has enough operations and success to gain the support of underwriters and the general market. You may owe some taxes as a result of waiting, but they can be substantially less than the taxes that will be due, if the stock price grows dramatically, as a result of trading on a national exchange.

So why not just buy the stock in the market, rather than deal with the taxes and restrictions of the early exercise of an option? That's a good question. Normally, the stock is not yet publicly traded, and ownership is limited to founders, wealthy, experienced investors, venture capital firms and a few employees. You—as an employee, director or independent contractor holding options—may be bullish about the future of the company and elect to take the risks associated with reverse vesting. If the stock pops, you have the opportunity to reduce your taxes, by avoiding an AMT adjustment on ISO's, getting long-term capital gains treatment on stock that is sold or deferring all taxes indefinitely, on stock that is held as a permanent part of your investment portfolio. On the other hand, if the company fails, never goes public or the stock value declines, you might lose some or all of your investment.

An Alternative to Stock Options

Some start-up companies use grants or sales of stock subject to resale agreements, as an alternative to help their key employees reduce the tax burden on their equity based compensation. This strategy will work only in limited situations, but it represents a powerful planning tool, under the right circumstances.

Sale with Substantial Restrictions

The stock value of a typical start-up company is very low. The company founders and initial investors generally own all of the stock, and there is no established market for any holder to sell his stock. Further, the company has little or no operating history or track record to assure its survival, much less any basis for projecting its future profitability. Thus, the value of a small minority block of stock, which you might acquire in a new company with no market liquidity, is highly discounted, from what might be a proportionate share of the company's net worth or future value.

Under such circumstances, a company may permit you to purchase stock at a nominal price that represents its current fair market value. The company has the option to allow purchases at a bargain price, as long as you include the bargain element in your income. Typically, the stock you purchase is subject to an escrow and resale agreement, under which you must resell the stock to the company, if you quit or are terminated within a certain time (for example, within three years). The resale obligations may expire on one date or may be phased out over time, in much the same ways in which stock options vest.

Properly structured, the resale agreement imposes a substantial risk of forfeiture on your ownership for purposes of Section 83 of the Internal Revenue Code. Because the stock is considered property under Section 83, you can make a Section 83(b) election and recognize income at the time of the purchase, rather than waiting until the terms of the resale agreement expire. Generally, there is little or no bargain element present at the time of the purchase, so little or no income is recognized, and little or no tax is due. The discussion of the Section 83(b) election in the preceding chapter is applicable to this strategy, and the tax benefits of establishing an early purchase date to qualify for the favorable long-term capital gains rates should be obvious.

Restricted Stock Financing Issues

There are two substantial disadvantages to employees in offerings of restricted stock sales. First, you are using your savings in a high-risk venture. Second, you may lack the financial resources to make the initial purchase and can't participate.

The first issue of high risk is generally unavoidable, due to the high failure rate of new companies. The risk of actually owning the stock outright is the price you pay, in an attempt to get long-term capital gains treatment and avoid a big tax at regular income tax rates. The amount invested is small in relation to the potential tax savings; however, you may be investing a large part of your net worth. If you are offered this option, you should seek professional advice to help balance the potentially onerous financial burden that comes (if the company fails) against the long-term benefits of making the early purchase.

The second issue might be addressed by arranging a loan for the purchase price of the stock. Creative minds immediately turn to non-recourse debt (where you are only obligated to deliver the collateral and are not personally liable for the loan) as a way to limit your risk. The Internal Revenue Service is aware of the concept and has indicated that it will generally consider stock purchased with non-recourse debt to be the equivalent of an option and ineligible for a Section 83(b) election. Consequently, the general rule (subject to some narrow exceptions that are beyond the scope of the discussion) is that you must be fully responsible for repaying loans used to purchase company stock, in order to make an early Section 83(b) election.

Companies are likely to use this strategy only with initial key employees because of these limitations. The most common approach will be a stock option plan (ISO or NSO) which permits early exercise subject to a resale agreement.

Chapter 3

Concentrated Stock Positions

Concentrated Stock Positions

We use the term concentrated stock position, to describe situations where your holdings in one or two stocks represent an unusually large percentage of your overall net worth. For example, you might have a total portfolio of $25 million, in which $20 million is invested in only one stock, and as a result, the majority of your wealth is "concentrated" in one security.

> Periodically, remind yourself that the darlings of today all too often are the duds of tomorrow. We have found that one of the most difficult parts of advising individuals, who have benefited from a highly appreciated stock, is getting them to have realistic expectations about the future.

If you have been fortunate enough to realize the benefits of concentration, you should work towards balancing the risks and rewards of holding a concentrated position. The simple *Rule of Seventy-Two* helps put things into perspective. You can simply divide 72 by the annual percentage yield expected, to estimate the number of years required to double your money (72/10% = 7.2 years to double, when earning 10% per annum).

The law of large numbers, diversification, and compounding give you alternatives to keep your assets working safely for you, without the elevated risks associated with concentrated positions. One look at the weekly price graphs of a couple of highflying stocks, and it is clear that there are benefits to protecting a portion of your unrealized gains. Periodically remind yourself that the darlings of today all too often are the duds of tomorrow. Just look at the price charts of a couple of companies where this happened.

GRAPH OF WEEKLY CLOSING PRICES OF QUALCOMM INCORPORATED

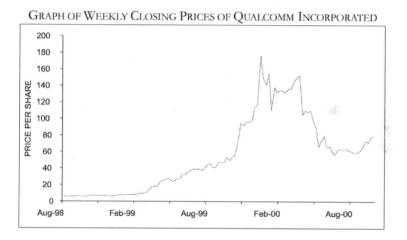

Figure 3.1

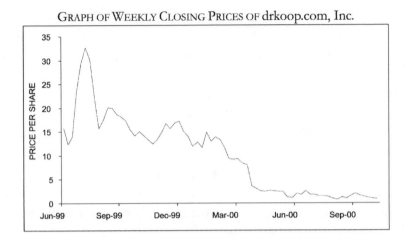

GRAPH OF WEEKLY CLOSING PRICES OF drkoop.com, Inc.

Figure 3.2

Investors have become wonderfully rich when a company has been highly successful, but they have also gone broke when the company failed and the stock lost its value. Generally, you are wise, to diversify your holdings and to spread your risk over several industries and a number of different companies. By so doing, you avoid the proverbial problem of having all of your eggs in one basket.

We have found that one of the most difficult parts of advising individuals who have benefited from a highly appreciated stock, is getting them to have realistic expectations about the future. Unfortunately, their emotions often outweigh reason, logic and historical evidence, until the inevitable happens.

Identifying Concentrated Positions

Concentrated positions are, in most cases, the result of a highly successful investment. It may have been the merger of a family business with a public company, the transition of a family business to a public company, through an initial public offering, the blossoming of one investment in a diversified portfolio, an inheritance, or for many employees of highly successful companies, the benefits of participating in a company stock option plan.

Concentrated positions—derived from stock option plans—frequently go through three development stages. The first is an unvested option to purchase stock with a relatively enormous value. The second phase is when the option is exercisable and/or vested. You must determine when it is best for you to exercise the option, how you will find the cash to pay the exercise price, and your best tax strategy. Finally, after exercising the options, you must figure out if it is wise to continue holding the concentrated position, or to implement an alternative strategy. There also may be company policy restrictions, agreements with underwriters, or federal security laws that prohibit you from selling the stock. When you have an unrestricted right to sell the stock, you should look for ways to diversify your holdings, in order to protect the economic benefits for yourself, your family, and any other beneficiaries of your wealth.

Wealth built on stock options tends to progress gradually, to a point of commonality with other concentrated stock positions, and, as a result, the latter portion of this book will follow this natural progression. Ultimately, we will look at strategies for managing wealth that is concentrated in one readily marketable security. These concepts and strategies are applicable to all concentrated positions, whether the position originated from a stock option or from any one of the other many beginnings.

Chapter 4

Rule 144 and Restricted Stock

Control Persons

Control persons (such as directors, executive officers, and shareholders owning 10% or more of the company stock) are prohibited from selling stock in the open market, except in compliance with the provisions of Rule 144. The determination of which executive officers are control persons is a legal matter, based upon the organizational structure of the company. In most cases, the company's general legal counsel is very cognizant of this issue and notifies the persons affected of their regulatory obligations. However, the ultimate responsibility for complying with the federal security laws lies with the officer, even if the company's lawyers do not help. Every individual serving as a senior officer in a public company should consult with the company's attorneys, or his own securities lawyer, concerning his obligations and duties under the federal and state securities laws.

IPO Lockup Agreements

Lockup agreements are contractual arrangements between a company and the underwriters of its shares that prohibit the sale of shares by some or all of the existing shareholders, for a period of time after an Initial Public Offering. Typically, holders of large blocks of stock, directors, and employees are prohibited from selling stock, for six months to one year after the IPO. The underwriters require the agreement to avoid downward price pressure that can come when existing shareholders flood the market with their holdings. Underwriters are also concerned about a perception that insiders have lost faith in their own company. The agreement is also intended to discourage key employees and founders from leaving the company and to maintain the continuity of the management team. Lock-up agreements protect the investors who purchase stock in the IPO, and, consequently, protect the underwriters' reputations for acting responsibly when offering investment securities to their clients.

Lockup agreements do not affect the vesting of ownership, for tax purposes. The AMT adjustment, for ISO's and the compensation element of NSO's on the bargain element, is computed without regard to a lock-up agreement.

You must inquire about lockup agreements and take them into account when planning the exercise of your options. You might invest a significant portion of your cash or create a large income tax liability by exercising options shortly after an IPO, but have little or no ability to defend against steep price declines during a lockup period. The results can be disastrous. For example, if you exercise a block of non-qualified stock options and rely on the sale of shares to pay the income taxes, you could lose everything if the stock declines by 60 percent during the lockup period.

Insider Information and Blackout Periods

Since the federal securities laws are primarily intended to assure adequate disclosure of all important information, it is illegal to use tips and inside information to gain an advantage in either the purchase or sale of a security. The person providing the tip, the person using the tip, and, many times, the company itself can be liable for fines and restitution to persons disadvantaged by disclosure of the information. Consequently, every public company and its employees must be careful in the timing of all purchases and sales of company stock, including stock acquired through the exercise of stock options. A sale of option stock immediately in advance of bad news will appear suspicious, even if the seller was totally unaware of the coming announcement. Consequently, some companies implement corporate policies prohibiting sales by key employees other than at set times. A company may also establish a blackout period, when stock sales are prohibited so as to avoid the appearance of impropriety. For example, a company may prohibit sales by key employees during the time between the end of a fiscal quarter and when the company publicly reports earnings.

You should obtain a clear understanding of current corporate policies on stock sales, and exercise care in avoiding circumstances having the appearance of improper use of inside information. An SEC investigation is burdensome for you, costing you substantial legal fees, exposing you to risk of jail time, and causing bad publicity for your company.

Section 16(b)

Section 16(b), the short swing profit rule of the Securities Exchange Act of 1934, applies to senior officers, directors, and shareholders owning 10% or more of the company stock, because of their special knowledge of inside information and their potential ability to manipulate the stock price.

The penalty provisions of Section 16(b) are triggered by either a purchase, followed by a sale within six months, or a sale, followed by a purchase within six months. A combination of any sale that can be matched with any purchase, within either the preceding or following six months will create liability.

Under the current Rule 16b–3, employers, by following certain prescribed procedures, exempt the grant of stock options from Section 16(b), in which case, the exercise of the option is not considered a *purchase*. Because Section 16(b) requires both a *purchase* and a *sale*, there can be no violation if the *purchase* element is missing. This means you can simultaneously exercise your options and sell the stock, without a Section 16(b) violation. Significantly, there is not an exemption for the actual sale of stock acquired by the exercise of an option. The sale of stock acquired by exercising an option can be matched with other purchases to trigger a Section 16(b) liability even though the purchase transaction is completely unrelated, such as participating in an Employee Stock Purchase Plan or making a purchase in the open market.

A Section 16(b) violation occurs when an executive sells some option stock, after he purchased shares in the open market within six months. Unfortunately, the executive will have to return all of the difference between the sale proceeds and the open market purchase price. An executive subject to Section 16(b) might be prohibited from selling stock for an extended time under circumstances where the shareholder is making periodic, unrelated purchases of the company stock.

Example: Jane purchases 10,000 shares of New Design Semiconductor, in the open market, for $7 per share on January 30, 2001. On June 15, 2001, she exercises her option, to purchase 15,000 shares at $5 per share and makes an immediate sale at $20 per share. Her sale of option shares creates a Section 16(b) violation because the purchase of 10,000 shares for $7 per share is within six months of her sale of an equal number of shares for $20 per share. Jane is liable to the company for $130,000 [10,000 x (20–7)].

Private Placement Purchases

Federal securities laws are designed to assure that certain minimum information is made available to investors, so they can make informed investment decisions. The foundation of these disclosure laws is a formal regulatory disclosure process that must be followed, whenever a company intends to issue and sell additional stock. Only stock that is purchased in connection with the formal disclosure procedure, called a *public offering*, may be resold to other investors in the open market.

The federal securities laws provide for the sale of unregistered securities. These are sales that are made without complying with the formal disclosure process of a public offering. The most commonly used is the *private placement*, which is based on the idea that certain investors are either smart enough or rich enough to take care of themselves. This exception is commonly used by start-up companies to raise capital from individuals, institutional investors, and venture capital groups. Stock purchased in these transactions can be resold only in another private placement, or under the provisions of Rule 144. This frequently includes stock acquired by founders and employees prior to the company's Initial Public Offering.

Rule 144: The Method for Selling Restricted Stock

Stock that is purchased in an unregistered offering (i.e., private placements), or is held by control persons, can be resold only under the provisions of Rule 144. Control persons are key officers, directors, and shareholders holding 10% or more of the company's outstanding shares. All company stock held by control persons is considered restricted, including shares acquired in a registered offering or purchased in the open market.

Most restricted stock bears a legend stating that it may be sold only in compliance with an exemption from the federal registration requirements and only upon approval of the sale transaction by the company's legal counsel. The restrictive legend serves to protect the company from allegations that it participated in an illegal scheme to sell its securities. A careful inspection of each stock certificate will usually alert a shareholder who holds restricted securities.

Rule 144 is designed to insure the public has current financial information concerning the company, to track the transactions by requiring reports to be filed with the SEC, and to limit the number of shares that may be sold during any three month period. The sale of restricted securities under Rule 144 must comply with the following conditions:

1. The shares were purchased and fully paid for, at least one year prior to the sale.

2. The seller files Form 144 with the SEC, no later than the day of the first sale. Effective for sales occurring within 90 days of the filing date, the information on Form 144 includes the number of shares the shareholder intends to sell and the reason for the sale.

3. The company has provided adequate current public information concerning its financial position. This requirement is usually satisfied with the filing of all the reports (Annual Form 10K and Quarterly Forms 10Q) required under the Securities Exchange Act of 1934.

4. The shares are sold in a *brokers' transaction*. This means there can be no active solicitation of purchase orders that are directly related to the sale of the restricted securities, and there can be no special commissions paid in connection with the sale.

5. If securities have been owned for a period of between one and two years, the number of shares sold ("dribbled out") is limited to the greater of 1% of the total outstanding shares or the average weekly trading volume for the four weeks preceding the date on which Form 144 is filed. Resale of shares held by non-affiliates for more than two years are not subject to the volume limitations; however, the number of shares sold by control persons is always subject to the volume restrictions.

Under the provisions of Rule 144(k), a person meeting the following qualifications is exempt from the volume limitations:

- Not an affiliate, at the time of sale
- Has not been an affiliate during the preceding three months, and
- Has held the stock for at least two years.

Remember, restricted stock usually has a legend, and a broker cannot enter an order to sell the stock until the legend has been removed. The rules for how and when a legend can be removed are complex, and many investors have unique situations that complicate the process; however, the process of having the legend removed, permanently or for a specific transaction, usually follows the following series of steps:

1. The shareholder notifies the company of his desire to make a sale or have the legend and the restrictions removed from his stock.

2. The company attorney provides a checklist of the documentation required. The list usually includes a requirement for the shareholder to hire an independent attorney to prepare a written opinion stating that the proposed sale or removal of the legend is permitted under the state and federal securities laws.

3. The shareholder's attorney conducts a due diligence inquiry concerning the facts and prepares the required opinion.

4. The company attorney reviews documentation provided by the shareholder and the opinion of counsel from the shareholder's attorney.

5. The company attorney approves the transaction and forwards the documentation to the company's transfer agent.

6. The company's transfer agent reviews the documentation and approves the transaction.

The restricted stock can be transferred only after *all* of the steps have been completed. This process is in addition to complying with Rule 144 and filing Form 144.

The process can take time, particularly the first time a shareholder makes a sale, and the wise investor will start the process well in advance of a desired sale date. Remember, the Form 144 filing is valid for 90 days, so there is no reason to wait until the last minute to start.

Rule 145

Under Rule 145, investors who are considered underwriters may resell stock received in certain business combinations (mergers, buy-outs, etc.) if specific conditions are met.

Rule 145 governs the sale of registered securities that are acquired by affiliates of a target company in a business combination. The general method of sale and second year volume restrictions of Rule 144 apply to most transactions. An investor who ceases to be an affiliate is released from the restrictions one year after the combination. Further, Rule 145 shares may under some circumstances be hedged or monetized, subject to certain volume restrictions.

This is the general rule, and as with all securities laws, the devil is in the details. You have the absolute legal responsibility to comply with the specific provisions of Rule 145, as they apply to your particular transaction and circumstances. Failure to comply can result in an SEC investigation and possible criminal charges. *Professional advice is not optional.*

Rule 701

Rule 701, commonly referred to as the private placement provision, allows small companies who do not report to issue stock in employee stock plans and other compensation plans without registering the securities.

Chapter 5

Other Related Tax Considerations

Taxes

Proper financial planning should include careful consideration of your taxes. Mandatory taxes can eat away the largest portion of your assets. There are federal income taxes, state income taxes, Medicare taxes, Social Security taxes, sales taxes, property taxes, gift taxes, estate taxes, sales taxes, and numerous others. At every corner, the taxman is waiting to collect his share of your money. You may work half your week just to pay taxes.

You can work your entire lifetime to acquire wealth and financial security for your family members only to have Uncle Sam take up to half of your estate when you die because you failed to plan properly.

You may feel you have no control, but in some situations, proper planning can dramatically reduce your tax burden, allowing you and your family to keep more of the money that you earn.

> **Example:** If you have a concentrated stock position, acquired through stock options and valued at ten million dollars, and can reduce your taxes from 39.6% to 20%, you can save nearly two million dollars.

Much of this book is devoted to explaining ways to turn ordinary income into long-term capital gains, thus cutting your tax bill in half. But below are other tax considerations that you should take into consideration. Each individual situation is unique and requires that you seek the help of qualified professionals.

Federal income taxes

Wash Sale Rules

The federal tax law defines a *wash sale* as the sale of a security at a loss when you make a purchase of an identical security within 30 days, either before or after the sale. The rule prevents you from recognizing paper losses for tax purposes, without actually disposing of the investment.

> **Example:** You purchase 100 shares of Lucent for $65 per share on June 10, 1999. You sell 100 shares on June 20, 2000, for $40 per share, and make a second purchase on July 18, 2000. This constitutes a wash sale, since there are fewer than 30 days between June 19, 2000 and July 18, 2000. Therefore, you cannot recognize the $25 per share loss.

Any purchase of an identical security, within a 61-day period surrounding the sale date, creates a wash sale. Count carefully. These are calendar days, and there is no room for a mistake.

A wash sale causes three consequences for you:

1. You are not allowed to claim the loss on the sale for the current tax year.
2. The disallowed loss is added to the basis of the replacement stock
3. The holding period for the stock that was sold is tacked onto the holding period for the replacement stock. If the original stock was held for six months and the replacement stock is held for seven months, the replacement is considered to have been held for thirteen months and qualifies for long-term capital gain treatment.

The basis adjustment preserves the long-term benefit of the disallowed loss. In most cases, the rules mean you will get the benefit of the loss later, rather than at the time of the original sale. There may be little or no effect, if the replacement stock is sold in the same year.

However, the sale of the replacement stock in a later year may be painful for the following reasons:

1. You may not get the benefit of large losses for many years, if you do not have capital gains to offset the losses; whereas, you may have large capital gains that are taxed for the year of sale.
2. If you die before selling the replacement stock, you permanently lose the loss deduction.
3. You may also permanently lose the loss deduction, if you try to avoid the wash sale rules, by purchasing the replacement property in your individual retirement account (IRA). There is little

authority on this issue, and nothing, to date, to prevent the Internal Revenue Service from taking such a position.

Among other things, the tacking on of the holding periods, for both the loss shares and the replacement shares, prevents you from converting a long-term capital loss into a short-term capital loss. It may also give you the benefit of long-term capital gains, in those circumstances where the investment quickly recovers and yields a positive overall return.

Short Sales

A traditional method, for protecting the value of concentrated or highly appreciated positions, was to make *short sales* of identical securities. If the value of the stock went down, the profit on the short sale was equal to the loss on the long-term position. The strategy was to pay tax on small to moderate price fluctuations, rather than tax on a much larger gain inherent in the highly appreciated shares. Changes in the tax laws, during recent years, have largely eliminated the benefits of this strategy, however:

1. A short sale is treated as a disqualifying disposition of ISO or ESPP stock.

2. A short sale terminates the holding period for identical stock held less than 12 months and can prevent you from getting long-term capital gains.

3. A short sale can be considered a *constructive sale* (defined later in this chapter) in the year of the short sale, rather than in a later year, when you dispose of the identical stock.

Generally, a short sale is a transaction, in which you sell borrowed stock, with the strategy of purchasing it later, at a lower price. You have an obligation to repay the borrowed stock at a later date. If you take a *short position* in a stock you make money when the stock goes down in value, and lose money when it goes up in value.

Since the amount of profit or loss is not known until the stock is purchased, there is no income tax on the sale proceeds. The income tax on the transaction is due for the year of sale.

You can sell a stock short, even when you already own the same shares. For example, you may own 500 shares of Coca Cola and want to sell 300 shares. You can either sell 300 shares in a customary transaction or make a short sale of 300 shares. If you make a short sale of stock, with securities you already own, the transaction is called going *short against the box.*

If you make a short sale of 300 shares against the box, you have neutralized the market fluctuations of that position, and before the tax law changes of recent years, delayed your tax liability until the position is closed by delivery of shares. You had further flexibility, in that you could choose to deliver either the existing shares or new shares, purchased at a much higher price solely for that purpose.

Adverse Consequences of Short Sales

Short sales, against the box of ISO or ESPP stock held less than the one and two year qualifying periods can be a disqualifying disposition. This means that you have compensation income at the time of the short sale, even if you use other stock to close the transaction.

A short sale terminates the holding period of stock that has not been held long enough to be taxed at long-term capital gains rates.

Example: You may have held a stock for 11 months, during which time it has doubled in value. You make a short sale against the box to protect the gain. Six months later, you buy new shares, to close the trade, and keep your original shares. The holding period for long-term capital gains purposes starts the day after the sale, and you will have to hold the original shares for an additional 12 months, in order to get the benefit of the long-term capital gains rates.

The law further provides that you are deemed to have made a constructive sale of stock, if you are short against the box. The constructive sale rules apply only to appreciated financial positions that will result in taxable gain, if sold outright. An exception is allowed if you:

1. Close your short position by January 30 of the year following the initial short sale

2. Continue to hold the original long position, without a protective short position for at least 60 days.*

Example: Jane holds 10,000 shares of NTC with a current market value of $50 per share and a cost basis of $5 per share. On May 12, 1999, Jane sells 10,000 shares of NTC short against the box. If Jane closes her short position by delivering shares on January 13, 2000, she will not be deemed to have made a constructive sale on May 12, 1999 so long as she does not open another protective short position for at least 60 days after closing the first.

If she makes a profit by purchasing new shares to close the short, she has to pay taxes on the difference between the sales price of

---

* QUERY: Can the long position be temporarily hedged with a put during the 60 day period and still qualify for the exception.

$50 per share on May 12 and the purchase price. If she has to pay more than the sales price to close the short, she generally has a non-deductible loss. The loss is added to the basis of the old shares since the short against the box position is usually considered a *straddle* (defined later in this chapter).

If Jane delivers the old shares before January 30, 2000, the sale is deemed to occur in 2000, and the gain on the disposition is included on her 2000 income tax return. This allows her to postpone the income taxes for one year.

Purchasing Put Options

You can protect the value of a stock position by purchasing a put option. An equity put option gives you the right to sell stock at a specific strike price, by a specific expiration date.

> **Example:** A put option, purchased in June, may give you the right to sell 100 shares of GE common stock for $50 per share, at anytime prior to the third Friday of the following August.

> If the price of GE shares goes above $50 per share, you lose the cost of the option. If the price of GE shares goes to $30 per share, you are protected against the loss, because you have the right to sell your shares for $50 per share.

However, the purchase of a put option, as a hedge on stock held less than 12 months, terminates the holding period, just like a short sale, and usually eliminates the desirability of this strategy. This can be particularly onerous for ISO or ESPP stock, where failure to meet the qualifying holding period results in compensation income. Further, the purchase of a put option, at a price equal to or greater than the market price of the shares, may cause a disqualifying disposition and result in compensation income, at the time of the purchase.

Straddles and Collars

The federal tax law defines *straddles* broadly, to include all strategies involving offsetting positions, with respect to a particular security. These are circumstances in which your risk of loss from one investment position is substantially diminished, by holding one or more other positions. A simple example is simultaneously holding both a put and a call on the same stock.

If you have a *straddle,* you cannot recognize any loss from closing one position, until the offsetting gain is recognized. In addition, any interest or other costs of establishing the position must be capitalized.

The rules are complex and far reaching, and you must be wary, when planning to hedge or protect the accumulated gain in an investment. The advice of seasoned and knowledgeable tax professionals is essential.

Constructive Sale

The Taxpayer Relief Act of 1997 designated a number of hedging or protective strategies as the equivalent of selling an original investment, in other words, a constructive sale. The essence of the new provisions is to require you to recognize the gain on an investment, at such time that you have effectively removed the risk of loss for continuing the investment.

Specifically designated are certain types of short sales, as discussed in a preceding section, *total return equity swaps,* and forward or future contracts that provide for a *substantially fixed amount* of an appreciated asset, in exchange for a *substantially fixed price*. In addition, *option collars* in which the put and call strike prices are too close to the market price (too tightly hedged) may be deemed a constructive sale, which creates an unintended taxable event.

The Internal Revenue Service has the authority to designate other similar risk hedging transactions as constructive sales. As yet, the Internal Revenue Service has not exercised its authority.

The rules are complex and the line between a permitted forward contract and one that creates a constructive sale is ambiguous. The often-repeated admonition clearly applies. Get good professional advice and guidance.

Identification of Shares

A stock position is frequently built over time, and the shares are frequently acquired through a number of separate transactions. Each block of stock may have a different cost basis and holding period. This situation can occur as your options vest and are periodically exercised. Consequently, if you sell part of your position, you may need to select the shares to be sold first. Picking the right shares to sell first can be critical, when dealing with compensation options.

> **Example:** You hold stock from the exercise of an ISO option granted 22 months prior to the sale and stock purchased in the open market 13 months prior to the sale. Sale of the stock, from the exercise of the ISO, will be a disqualifying disposition and all of the gain will be compensation income, taxed at ordinary income tax rates. Gain on the sale of the stock purchased in the open market and held more than 12 months will be taxed at long-term capital gains rates. You can pay an enormous amount

of unnecessary tax, if you fail to properly identify the stock purchased in the open market as the shares to be sold.

When there are multiple acquisition dates and cost bases, the tax law permits you to identify specific shares to be sold. The choice must be made at the time of the sale, or you are deemed to have selected the shares on a *first-in-first-out basis.*

If you have chosen to hold the physical certificates for the stock, you must make your choice by selecting the certificate to deliver to your broker in settlement of the trade. The more common practice is to have your broker hold all the shares in a single account. When you're ready to sell stock, you must identify a certain block with your broker, at the time of sale, and obtain written confirmation of the specification, within a reasonable time after the sale. In most cases, the identification is by purchase date, and is recorded on the confirmation received from your broker following the trade. Make certain you get the written confirmation and retain it with your tax records.

If you hold stock in several accounts, you should take care that the shares you identify have in fact been deposited into the account.

> **Example:** If you deposit shares from the exercise of an ISO in one account and shares purchased in the open market in another account, you will have difficulty, if you prematurely sell the shares from the ISO account, when you intend to sell the shares acquired in the open market.

On the other hand, you may get some automatic identification of shares and avoid much heartache, by keeping ISO shares in an account separate from those purchased in the open market.

Federal Estate Taxes

A Dual Tax System

The federal tax system of the United States can be both confusing and irritating to its citizens. One source for that confusion is the parallel and partially overlapping nature of the income tax system and estate tax systems.

Generally, the federal law imposes an income tax when wealth is acquired, and charges either a gift tax or estate tax when wealth is transferred to the next generation.

> **Example:** If you are accumulating wealth through employee stock options, you frequently will pay income tax on the exercise of the options. Subsequent sales of the stock can create additional short-term capital gain or long-term capital gain tax on the appreciation. If you decide to give the stock or cash from the sale to your descendents, you must follow the rules of the federal gift tax system and may owe an additional gift tax (a second tax) on the transfer. Further, any property transferred by will, at death, is subject to an estate tax. If you die while holding NSO options, your family can easily lose 70% of their value through the combination of estate taxes and income taxes.

The systems are not entirely independent and, with careful planning, you may escape one level of taxation or significantly reduce each level of taxation.

The Unified Transfer Taxes

The gift tax and estate tax are coordinated, so that gifts made during a person's lifetime can affect the amount of estate tax paid at the time of the individual's death.

To understand this unified system for taxing transfers, we will begin with the gift tax system. Generally, a gift tax is not due until you make cumulative gifts of more than $675,000 during your lifetime. (The $675,000 lifetime exemption is scheduled to gradually increase to $1,000,000 by the year 2010.) Every year, an individual is required to file a gift tax return, to report all gifts other than those specifically excluded from disclosure and taxation. A record of each individual's history must be retained and the gifts for the current year are combined with all taxable gifts, during prior years, to compute a tax on the cumulative total. The Unified Gift and Estate Tax Table, as follows, shows the tax rates for transfers, during the year 2000:

Unified Gift & Estate Tax Table

Column A	Column B	Column C	Column D
Taxable amount over	Taxable amount not over	Tax on amount in Column A	Rate of tax on excess over amount in Column A
-	10,000	0	18
10,000	21,000	1,800	20
21,000	40,000	3,800	22
40,000	60,000	8,200	24
60,000	80,000	13,000	26
80,000	100,000	18,200	28
100,000	150,000	23,800	30
150,000	250,000	38,800	32
250,000	500,000	70,800	34
500,000	750,000	155,800	37
750,000	1,000,000	248,300	39
1,000,000	1,250,000	345,800	41
1,250,000	1,500,000	448,300	43
1,500,000	2,000,000	555,800	45
2,000,000	2,500,000	780,800	49
2,500,000	3,000,000	1,025,800	53
3,000,000	***	1,290,000	55

Figure 5.1

The tax rates start at 37% and increase as the aggregate amount of your lifetime gifts accumulate; you will eventually pay a tax equal to as much as 55% of a gift to a friend or family member.

Mechanically, a tax is computed each year for the cumulative gifts subject to the tax, and only the tax attributable to the current year transfers must be paid. Further, each individual is given a lifetime credit equal to the amount of tax that would otherwise be charged on the first $675,000 of gifts.

> **Example:** The gift tax liability, at the end of 2000, of a person who makes a gift of $700,000 in 1999 and another gift of $200,000 in 2000, would be computed as follows:

Simplified computation:

The total tax that would be due if all $900,000 were transferred in 2000	86,250
Less: The tax that was paid on the 1999 gifts of $700,000	(18,500)
Tax due for 2000	67,750

Illustration of more detailed computation:

Gift in 2000		200,000
Prior Gifts (1999)		700,000
Total cumulative gifts		900,000
Tax on cumulative gifts ($900,000)	306,800	
Unified credit (equal to tax on first $675,000 of gifts)	(220,550)	86,250
Tax on prior gifts of $700,000 (1999)	229,800	
Unified credit used in 1999 (equal to tax on $650,000)	(211,300)	18,500
Tax due on 2000 gifts		67,750

At death, the assets in an individual's estate are added to the gifts during the decedent's lifetime, and the estate tax is computed in much the same manner as in the example above. The gifts, during a decedent's lifetime, are part of the cumulative transfers and serve to both push the estate into higher tax brackets and use up the lifetime gift and estate tax credit.

Many times, wealthier individuals will use the unified credit during their lifetime, to get a rapidly appreciating asset out of their estate with the lowest possible gift and estate tax cost. This strategy can backfire if the asset unexpectedly becomes worthless, or if the step-up in basis for income tax purposes is more important than appreciation of the asset. Using the unified credit during your lifetime should be a part of an overall tax plan that is designed with the advice and guidance of a skilled tax professional.

Gifts of Less than $10,000

You can give $10,000 per donee, per year, without paying a gift tax or including the gift in your cumulative lifetime gifts. A married couple can give $20,000 per donee ($10,000 from the husband plus $10,000 from the wife).

This exclusion applies only to gifts of a present interest, typically a simple, unrestricted transfer of title. However, many parents and grandparents want to place the gift in trust, because the donee is a minor, prone to unwise decisions, or in order to protect the asset against the claims of spouses and creditors. A gift to a trust can be treated as a present interest, if the beneficiary has the right to withdraw the gift—or assets of equivalent value—from the trust, for a limited time following the gift. You will need to have a tax attorney prepare the trust document and advise you on the procedures to follow for each gift, if you want to prevent your gifts to a trust from being disqualified as a future interest.

Over time, if you have multiple donees (as a grandparent often does), you can move substantial wealth out of your estate, without incurring any gift or estate taxes. It pays to start early with your estate planning.

> **Example:** A grandmother with 20 grandchildren can move $200,000 (20 x $10,000 each) out of her estate each year, without paying any gift taxes or effecting her estate tax liability. The amount moved will be double, if her husband is alive and participates in the gift plan.

The Qualified State Tuition Plans (also called Section 529 Plans) allow a grandparent to use this exclusion to put $50,000 per grandchild ($100,000 for couples), gift tax free, into a college fund. The funds grow on a tax-deferred basis, until the beneficiary withdraws the money to pay qualified educational expenses. The growth is taxed at the beneficiary's tax rate, when withdrawn. The grandmother, in the above example, could move $1,000,000 ($50,000 x 20) out of her estate. The rules of Section 529 require her to survive the gift by five years, to get the full benefit of the exclusion.

Other Exclusions

In addition to the $10,000 annual exclusion, you can make unlimited gifts and bequests to your spouse (tax free transfers are limited to $100,000, if your spouse is not a United States citizen). As with the annual exclusion, technical tax rules must be followed, if the transfer is to a trust rather than a simple, unrestricted transfer of title. Among other things, the spouse must be entitled to all income during the spouse's lifetime, a special election must be made on a timely filed gift or estate tax return, and the assets will be included on the spouse's gift or estate tax return, if subsequently transferred in a taxable transaction. Again, a skilled tax attorney must prepare the trust document and each step of the transaction should be taken with the attorney's guidance and supervision.

Payment of educational and medical expenses is excluded from the definition of taxable gifts, if the payments are made directly to the service provider. This can be a particularly powerful strategy for grandparents with a large second generation that is pursuing advanced degrees at private universities.

> **Example:** A couple can give $20,000 to a grandchild and pay $35,000 of room and board at a private university. The entire $55,000 is excluded, for gift and estate tax purposes.

Estate Planning

Many individuals have achieved a level of financial success that enables them to fulfill their personal goals, without exhausting their assets.

> Often, successful people work their entire lives to build an estate of great value and then neglect to invest a tiny fraction of that time to protect it, through proper estate planning.

Neglect of proper estate planning may result in the government getting more of the estate than the families or charities you wish to support. Here are examples where this happened to well known individuals.

Example of Poor Estate Planning

Person	Gross Estate	Settlement Costs	Net Estate	Percentage Shrinkage
Elvis Presley	$ 10,165,434	$ 7,374,635	$ 2,790,799	73%
J.P. Morgan	17,121,482	11,893,691	5,227,791	69%
John Rockefeller	26,905,182	17,124,988	9,780,194	64%
Marilyn Monroe	819,176	448,750	370,426	55%

Figure 5.3

Estate planning is a complex, interdisciplinary process that should be individually tailored to achieve the unique goals of each individual. These goals are as widely varied and individually unique as the personal circumstances of each person in our society. It is impossible to create or apply a single formula. You should design a plan to leave your assets to the people or organizations you choose, and to make certain your assets will be left in a way that enhances the quality of life, for those people who benefit from the fruits of your lifetime of work and stewardship.

Good estate planning requires access to specialized technical knowledge in taxes, life insurance, trusts, investment planning and a whole host of other topics. Many estate plans are successfully executed, only if the plan is administered in complete compliance with highly technical rules. One simple, good faith error can badly disrupt a great plan. For this reason, estate planning is not suitable for home remedies or do-it-yourself projects. The cost of skilled professional advice is cheap, when compared with the cost of inadvertent errors and lost opportunities.

PART II

Stock Options and Concentrated Stock Position Strategies

Chapter 6

Personalized Planning and Goal Setting

Starting with the End in Mind

This is probably the most important part of the book. Most people make financial decisions based on feelings of fear or greed or on what they have heard or believe, without any logical reasoning. Some get lucky gambling on stocks, but the majority loses a great deal, if they do not understand the dynamics and the laws of the market.

If you do not know where you are going, it will be hard to get there. It is like building a house without a blueprint or taking a road trip without a map or clear destination. It is crucial that you have clear goals when dealing with your personal finances. All choices and decisions should be designed to help you achieve your objectives and dreams in the most efficient and effective manner. Asset allocation, tax planning, and risk management strategies should be customized to match your uniqueness as an investor.

Setting Goals That Match Your Personal Values and Needs

Investment management and financial planning should not be done in a vacuum, but rather should mesh closely with your—and your family's—fundamental values. Both you and your financial advisor benefit from candid discussions of your true goals and objectives, at the beginning of your relationship. Your advisor's attentive and sincere interest, in understanding you, will come only through a series of thoughtful questions that will help in the design of an appropriate strategy. These questions will require you to make choices and to confront the vagueness of your thoughts. Finally, the verbal articulation of your values, dreams, and desires will sharpen your focus and help solidify a commitment to those specific life paradigms.

It is critical that you establish goals that match your personal values. Goals in this context are estimates of specific amounts of money, in lump sum or in periodic payments, which are needed to support your chosen lifestyle or to purchase the tangible items that you want or need. You should prioritize those goals and write them down, in order of the most important to the least.

You and your advisors can then design a written disciplined strategy that will ensure that, over time, you will realize your goals and, perhaps, many of your grandest dreams.

Several things influence your investment profile: the assets you have at the beginning and the amount necessary to achieve your goals, the amount of time you have to grow your financial resources, the severity of the consequences of not achieving your goals, and your ability to emotionally and psychologically withstand significant fluctuations in the value of your investments. The following general goals are frequently used as a beginning place for structuring an investment portfolio.

Preserve capital

As the most conservative goal, your principle objective is to preserve your assets and minimize your risks. You are willing to accept low returns, in an effort to minimize risk. Typical investment vehicles might include cash, certificates of deposits, treasury notes and short-term high-quality bonds.

Generate current income

Your main concern is to have your assets provide a safe and continuing stream of income payments from very dependable investments. You should be willing to handle the modest fluctuation in portfolio value associated with changes in fixed income pricing, as interest rates fluctuate. Typical investments are cash, short and long-term, mid to high quality bonds, and stable dividend producing stocks.

Generate income and growth

You seek a balanced portfolio, in order to receive current income, from bonds and dividends, but you're also willing to assume some risk, in order to obtain appreciation of your portfolio. Investments may include a diversified portfolio of short and long-term bonds, equities, and other assets.

Achieve long-term growth

You have a three-to five-year time horizon and are interested in accumulating wealth, rather than income. You are willing to accept a degree of risk and volatility, due to your exposure in the stock market. Continued contributions, dollar cost averaging, and dividend reinvestments should increase future value. The majority of your portfolio is allocated in stocks, but assets such as zero-coupon bonds, and other vehicles can be used to take advantage of opportunities and increase overall returns.

Achieve aggressive growth

Your goal is to achieve above-average rates of return over a three-to five-year period and you are willing to take on substantial risks and principle volatility. Your portfolio may be over weighted in certain sectors and the investor is normally active in shifts in and out of positions.

Maximize capital appreciation

Your primary objective is to maximize the total return of your portfolio, within a one year period. This is certainly the riskiest goal and normally has the highest degree of volatility and activity. Your portfolio may have concentrated positions, equity options, and other assets that you feel will work to achieve abnormal returns in the short term.

Concentration vs. Diversification

Concentration creates wealth, and diversification protects it. The wealth of many people around us seems to have been created overnight, but it can also vanish in a very short period of time if individuals fail to protect that wealth. It is often very difficult for an individual, who has watched his net worth increase by millions, very quickly, to be rational and to shift gears from wealth accumulation to wealth preservation. Many such investors naively believe that their beloved stock is different from others and will only continue to soar, but too often, greed and arrogance blinds them to the uncalculated gamble they are taking.

Example: A few months ago a gentleman, we will call Jim, was referred to us, because he had options at his biotech company that were worth several million dollars. After a few short conversations on the phone, he came in. We briefly discussed the risks involved in holding his options, but he was unwilling to spend the time required for us evaluate his situation. After all, he had recently attended a meeting with the CEO, who assured the sales force that the stock would continue to soar. Jim was very confident about the future of the company and not interested in any strategies to protect his position. He was in a hurry, so we set an appointment to meet again. Unfortunately, he cancelled it and never rescheduled. Over the next couple of months, we watched his stock drop from a high of $167 to as low as $55 dollars a share. His wife, who had originally initiated our first conversation, was unhappy, and Jim does not feel quite as smart as he did just a few months ago.

Jim failed to shift gears from accumulation to preservation, from *getting* rich to *staying* rich. Consequently, he and his family literally lost millions.

Asset Allocation

Studies have shown that, over time, how your assets are allocated dictates more than 92% of the total return of a portfolio. This fact is commonly overlooked, while individuals and some professionals look for the next lottery stock. It's funny how the local news always puts the one winner of the lottery on the TV for everyone to see, but they ignore the millions who lost at the same game. *The bottom line is that asset allocation is the most critical part of your portfolio.*

The goal of asset allocation is to minimize risk and to maximize return on your portfolio, so that you might reach your individual goals in the most efficient manner.

The following graph—of the efficient investment frontier—illustrates the importance of having the right mix to optimize risk and reward over the long run. If you have a large portfolio, you should work to *over*weight sectors that are projected to have high growth rates or that are undervalued, and work to *under*weight sectors that are grossly over valued or have little to no growth rates. Asset allocation is driven by your risk tolerance.

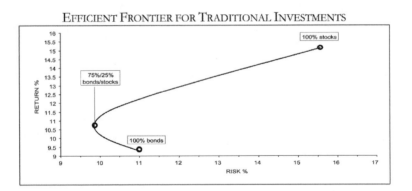

Figure 6.1

The Markowitz Model illustrating the efficient frontier demonstrates the efficiency created by mixing different asset classes. His goal and the goal of many asset managers is to find the most efficient point in a port-folio that maximizes total return while minimizing risks. This goal is achieved with the optimal amount of asset classes, and based on an individuals risk tolerance.

As you can see in the graph above, a portfolio with 100% stocks may yield the highest return over the long run, but also has the highest degree of risk. A portfolio with 100% bonds will have the lowest level of volatility and risk, but also the lowest rate of return. The most efficient point and optimal risk-return relationship can be found with the proper amount of stocks and bonds. In the example above, an individual depending on his risk tolerance would attempt to structure a portfolio that returns the appropriate rate based on the amount of risk assumed. Therefore, your objective would be to take only the risks that you are rewarded for. The graph clearly illustrates the advantage in risk/reward efficiency of holding a portfolio of 25% stocks and 75% bonds versus a portfolio of all bonds.

A Written Plan to Guide You, Your Family and Your Advisors

If you are pitching a tent, you may not have to look at the directions, but if you are building your dream home, which you plan to live in for the rest of your life, it is critical to meet with an architect, to develop a very specific blueprint to ensure that your house is built correctly. The same thing applies to your finances. After you clarify your goals, you should develop a written plan, a comprehensive financial plan, that will instill structure and discipline and will address everything that is important to you.

Building a Team of Experts and Specialists

Your financial team should include an investment adviser, a CPA, an attorney, and an insurance professional. Your team should be skilled and knowledgeable in asset allocation, investment selection, income tax, estate tax, life insurance, trusts, and estate administration, to guide you in creating your plan and to handle the technical details required to put your plan into motion. As we have said earlier, this process is not well suited to home remedies or do-it-yourself approaches. The peace of mind and other benefits of a skilled professional team outweigh the costs.

Chapter 7

Option Management Strategies For ISO's

Overview

Because stock options may constitute a large percentage of your net worth, options must be handled with extreme caution. Taxes and falling share prices are two main culprits that can cost you thousands, and in many cases, millions of dollars. Careful tax, legal and financial planning is essential to protect against unnecessary risks and taxes.

If you are holding a significant block of stock options, you should be asking a number of questions.

1. How should I manage the risks associated with options?
2. How should I pay for the stock and the taxes when I choose to exercise the options?
3. What should I do with the stock, once the options are exercised?

Again, *you do not own the stock, until you exercise your options*; at which time, you may have a concentrated position, if you do not sell the stock. At a minimum, you should consider the following few basic strategies:

1. Exercise and sell
2. Partial exercise to cover costs
3. Installment exercises
4. Postpone or hold for the full option term
5. Exercise and hold

Exercise and Sell

Your decision, to exercise a block of options and immediately sell, is usually the result of an immediate cash need or the desire to diversify your investments. This is particularly important, if you have reason to fear a sudden decline in price. While not the most efficient tax strategy, this choice may prove desirable, when the rate of return on the investments, selected to achieve diversification, is more than the rate of appreciation for the stock, especially, when the return from the diversified portfolio is achieved with less risk than what would be experienced by holding a concentrated position.

The taxation is straightforward. You are making a disqualifying disposition, so the difference between the exercise price and the sales price is ordinary income received as compensation for services. There is no AMT adjustment, when the shares are sold in the same year as the option is exercised.

Example: Jane holds options to purchase 15,000 shares of NDS for $5 per share. The stock has traded as high as $150 per share and is trading for $100 per share. Jane's options represent her entire net worth, and she is concerned about the value of the company stock over the next year. She elects to exercise her options and immediately sell the stock. She gets a net $860,700, after taxes, which is invested in a well-diversified portfolio to grow at 10% to 13% per year. Jane has executed a strategy to build a sound financial foundation that will continue to grow, until her retirement. In her case, she held additional options that vest and become exercisable over the next four years. She will continue to participate in the future growth of her employer, but with substantially less risk.

Planned Installment Exercises For Tax Efficiency

Planning for incentive stock options is largely a matter of timing, to gain tax efficiency.

Traditional planning focuses on timing the exercise of options, to minimize the alternative minimum tax (or to maximize the credit in subsequent years), and to maximize the portion of the profit taxed at long-term capital gains.

Spread Exercises Over Several Years

Most traditional planning focuses on spreading the exercise of options and subsequent stock sales over several years, to avoid or minimize the net cost of the AMT. The rate of exercise is determined by size of the bargain element, the number of options exercised relative to your individual tax position, and a number of other factors that will be unique to only you. In some cases, you may be able to exercise all of your options, as soon as allowed, without incurring AMT, but in others, some AMT burden may be inevitable. Effective planning requires preparation of pro-forma estimates of your income tax liability for the year of exercise, the year of sale, and all years in between.

Enhanced Opportunities to Manage Portfolio

Your flexibility in planning is extremely limited when holding unexercised ISO's. An early exercise and sale gives maximum opportunity to reduce the investment risk, but at a high cost. You give up the financial leverage of the interest free loan and pay the highest applicable tax rates. The installment purchase strategy also gives up the interest free loan, but works to get the best tax efficiency, by minimizing the tax burden on your options. In addition to minimizing taxes, the installment exercise strategy gives greater flexibility in making investment decisions.

Maximum flexibility comes once you have exercised an option and held the stock long enough to avoid a disqualifying disposition and gain the benefits of the long-term capital gains rates.

- The stock can be sold, with minimum tax costs, and your portfolio can be diversified.
- A concentrated position can be hedged with sophisticated investment strategies.
- Income tax can be reduced through the use of charitable remainder trusts.
- Estate taxes can be managed through use of trusts, partnerships, gift programs and other sophisticated strategies.

Paying for the Shares and the Taxes

One strategy, for you, is to exercise and sell enough stock to cover the total exercise price of the options and any other related expenses. By electing to sell enough to cover the costs, you own the resulting net stock, without incurring interest expense from borrowing to purchase the stock, and are able to convert short-term gains tax into long-term capital gains tax on the resulting stock, if desired. You may choose this strategy if your options are nearing expiration and you need to purchase the stock without using other assets, or if you're unwilling to increase your risks by borrowing to exercise the options.

You may want to borrow money to pay the initial exercise price. In many cases, brokers will readily loan you the money you need to pay the exercise price. A contractual agreement, among the brokerage firm, your employer, and you, allows the brokerage firm to advance the exercise price and to hold the shares as collateral for the purchase money loan. Typically, this is arranged as a margin loan, and it is subject to security industry rules requiring you to maintain certain minimum equity in a collateral account. The sections on managing concentrated stock positions outline methods for managing the risk associated with a margin account.

Not everyone is comfortable with using borrowed money for an extended time to exercise options and to pay the resulting taxes. Tax efficiency can still be achieved by use of careful timing. Proceeds from shares, purchased in the first quarter of the current year and sold during the first quarter of the next, can meet the holding period, for long-term capital gains, and still be available to retire the purchase money loan and pay the extra taxes due, on account of the exercise. The gain on the exercise, the difference between the sales price and the exercise price, will be taxed at a maximum of 20% for federal purposes, rather than the much higher ordinary income rates of up to 39.6%. In the alternative, shares of an ISO, which have been held for more than 12 months, can be used to exercise the options in an IRC §1036 tax sheltered exchange.

In some cases, you can exercise a portion of your options and hold the shares long enough to get the benefit of long-term capital gains rates. The shares are sold as soon as they meet the required holding period. This is a rather simple manipulation of the tax rates. The timing and amount of ISO options, subsequently exercised, may be adjusted in order to take advantage of the extra income generated by the sale of shares for purposes of the AMT calculation.

> **Example:** You may exercise options on 1,000 shares this year, and sell the underlying stock 12 months later, in the next tax year. The extra taxable income, from the regular tax gain on the sale of the stock, may permit you to make subsequent exercises in the second year without incurring an AMT.

Postpone or Hold for the Full Option Term

Holding an option for the full term of the agreement is often thought to be one of the best ways to maximize its potential value. You would postpone exercise or hold the option, if you were very bullish in the stock or wanted to delay your taxes. An option gives you the equivalent of an interest free loan, for the amount of the exercise price. Holding an option for its full term maximizes your financial leverage. When a stock option is exercised, you must pay the actual cost of purchasing the shares, and in some cases, an alternative minimum tax. This payment must be in cash, from your savings, or, in some cases, it may be acquired through the immediate sale of shares. Sales reduce the number of shares you hold for future appreciation; therefore, the amount that is paid to the government and the corporation is no longer working for you. This is frequently called an opportunity cost, and the amount of compound appreciation sacrificed over time can be tremendous.

The main reason for waiting as long as possible to exercise an option is that this strategy does not require a cash outlay from you.

Risk of Unprotected Position

Holding options for the full term has both systemic risks—general market fluctuations—and non-systemic risks—risks unique to your company. You might hold millions of dollars in equity from your options' bargain element, but the price of the underlying stock, many times, will go down as fast as it went up. You may have to wait years to recover your equity and will lose everything if the options are under water when they expire.

In early 2000, many high tech optionees watched millions of dollars of option equity vanish overnight. Investment professionals found a common thread, in that these optionees, who had limited market experience, also had unrealistic expectations from their company stock. In many cases, they put off planning too long. Greed and lack of knowledge about historical market performance costs many investors a large portion of their net worth. Don't become one of them.

Another risk, commonly overlooked by some of these optionees until it was too late, is the risk of being terminated and losing the right to their options, which may have a large bargain element.

Understanding your company plan is important to fully knowing what you have at risk.

> **Example:** We recently heard of an individual who was fired for sexual harassment, and lost all rights to his unexercised stock options. The bargain element was in the millions, and he is in an extremely difficult financial position.

Estate Tax Considerations

If you elect to hold your options for the full term, before exercising, you may be confronted with a difficult estate tax problem, assuming the value of the options is substantial. In many cases, this can be tens of millions of dollars.

Many option plans, both ISO and NSO, will accelerate the vesting schedule, and require an exercise of the option within a limited time following death, such as one year. The acceleration of ISO's can cause the aggregate exercise price of options, first exercisable in the year of your death to exceed $100,000, thus converting ISO's to NSO's. In addition, the exercise of substantial ISO's is likely to result in an alternative minimum tax liability. Finally, the exercise of NSO's certainly carries the heavy burden of an immediate tax on the bargain element. Generally, there will be a heavy income tax burden of one form or another soon after your death, and the tax rate can be as high as 39.6%.

Further, the transfer of your options and the underlying stock to beneficiaries, other than in a unified credit shelter trust or to your spouse, can incur an estate tax as high as 55%. While your estate may get an income tax deduction for the estate tax, the overall burden can run as high as 70%.

Finally, if you have options with cumulative values far in excess of what you need for your support, you have limited options for transferring the future appreciation to your beneficiaries, as long as you continue to hold non-transferable options.

Comprehensive estate planning can address these issues, through combinations of life insurance and trusts having special provisions to minimize your estate tax burdens. In some cases, the estate tax burden may encourage you to exercise options, rather than continue to hold them for the full term.

Exercise and Hold

If you are bullish on a stock and your options are nearing expiration, you might elect to commit the funds to buy the stock and then hold it, in anticipation of future appreciation. Your opportunity cost would be the amount you could have earned on the assets that were used to pay for the stock. If you are not affected by AMT, you will only be out the exercise price and any transaction costs associated with the exercise. You may use the cash, or a portion of the shares, to cover the costs.

Exercising and holding is rather risky, if your concentrated position is unprotected. (Later, strategies to protect a concentrated position are discussed.) If you used other non-related assets to purchase the shares, your overall commitment and risk has increased. More risk should be accepted only when compensated by an opportunity for greater financial reward.

Focus on Special Times to Exercise

You should pay particular attention to your tax planning at the beginning and end of each year. December 31 is the last opportunity for you to exercise any options in the current year. Any opportunity to save taxes, by exercising in the current calendar year, will be irrevocably lost at the end of the day.

Exercising options early in the year, before April 15, allows you to satisfy the 12-month holding period, before the tax is due the next year. This is one strategy that allows investors more time to obtain the cash to pay a large AMT liability.

> **Example:** Jane exercises her ISO's to purchase 15,000 shares NTC for $5 per share on January 20, 1999, when the market price is $100 per share. She has an alternative minimum tax of $398,479, due on April 15, 2000.
>
> Jane has the choice of selling stock prior to December 31,1999, as a disqualifying disposition, in the current year (taxed at 39.6%), or holding the stock, until after January 20, 2000, to recognize all of the bargain element as a long-term capital gain (taxed at 20%). While the best tax answer might seem obvious, from the above rules, Jane must hire a tax expert to advise her, because the AMT rules create surprising answers. In many cases, Jane pays the same amount of taxes, regardless of her choice between an immediate sale or holding for long-term capital gains treatment.

You do not have this opportunity if your options are exercised later in the year. You will either have to make a disqualifying disposition, borrow the money, or fund any AMT liability from another source.

This strategy works only if the two-year holding period is also satisfied by the date of the sale in the second calendar year.

Another reason to exercise early in the year is to gain flexibility in responding to a declining stock price. In cases, where the stock price has declined below the fair market value on the exercise date, you may avoid the AMT capital loss limitation. A fairly obscure rule limits the AMT loss, when combined with other gains and losses, to $3,000. This limitation can prevent you from utilizing the AMT credit, and can arise even if you make a disqualifying disposition. A special rule allows you to escape the AMT capital loss limitation, for shares sold at a loss in the same year as acquired, by the exercise of an option.

If you exercise your ISO in January, you have eleven months to see if a decline in value will trap you with the AMT capital loss limitation. If the problem arises, you have until December 31 (eleven months) to sell the shares and escape. By contrast, an exercise in December gives you very limited time to react.

Early Exercise and Hold of ISO's—Section 83(b) Elections

The so-called Reverse Vesting plans combine an ISO (or NSO) with a restrictive contract on the shares acquired through the exercise of the option. Since the contract requires you to resell the shares to your company, in the event you terminate the relationship, Section 83 provides for deferral of any compensation income, until the restrictions lapse. However, since the shares are property, for purposes of Section 83, you can make a Section 83(b) election, to recognize the bargain element as income at the time the shares are acquired, rather than when the restrictions lapse.

This strategy is used primarily when the option price is equal to or near the exercise price, when the exercise price is nominal, as compared with the expected long-term appreciation, and when you can comfortably make the financial investment in the shares or have access to the necessary liquidity.

An early exercise of an ISO option can significantly reduce or eliminate the AMT liability. This strategy is most frequently used for options issued by private start-up companies. The ISO rules require the exercise price to be equal to the fair market value on the date of grant. If the option is immediately exercised, there is no AMT adjustment. This also starts the holding period for purposes of qualifying for the long-term capital gains tax rates.

> **Example:** Assume Jane holds ISO's, to purchase 50,000 shares
> of NTC company stock for $1 per share, and the plan gives her
> the option to purchase the shares on the grant date, subject to
> a resale obligation. If Jane immediately exercises the option,
> she can make a Section 83(b) election, without any AMT lia-
> bility, because the exercise price and the market value are the
> same. If the company goes public two years later, after Jane has
> met the required holding periods (two years from grant, one
> year from exercise), she will be able to sell the stock and qual-
> ify for long-term capital gains treatment, as soon as the lock-
> up agreement with the underwriters expires. Alternatively, she

can hold the stock indefinitely, without worrying about a big AMT liability upon exercise or about the options expiring. Finally, her unrestricted ownership gives her complete flexibility to use any of the sophisticated strategies for managing concentrated stock positions.

Chapter 8

Option Management Strategies For NSO's

Overview

Many factors should be considered when choosing a strategy that is right for you. The decision should not be strictly based on the financial forecasts and on monetary elements. It is sad, but true, that most investors make decisions based on emotions, rather than on logic and reason; therefore, it is prudent to try to find some balance. If the majority of your net worth in tied up in one company, and you are worried about losing almost everything, why not exercise a portion, so that you can have some security and piece of mind? Remember the axiom, "A bird in the hand is worth two in the bush."

Many strategies and issues discussed in Chapter 7, on ISO's, are the same or very similar to the strategies and issues for NSO's. A key difference is when the taxes on the bargain element must be paid. If AMT does not apply when exercising ISO's, you are not responsible for the taxes until you elect to transfer or sell the stock. On the other hand, if you exercise NSO's, you are responsible for paying ordinary income tax on the bargain element when the option is exercised. Therefore, ISO's and NSO's have very different tax implications to you as an investor.

Exercise and Sell at Earliest Opportunity

As an option holder, you may follow an exercise and sell strategy for NSO's for much the same reason as for ISO's, and accordingly, the ISO discussion is generally applicable to the strategy for NSO's.

The taxation of an exercise and sell strategy is straightforward. You must pay a 28% withholding tax and the applicable Social Security/Medicare tax to your company. The bargain element on the exercise date is taxed as compensation, at ordinary income tax rates, and the balance of any tax in excess of the withholding paid to the company, is due on your individual income tax return (or through quarterly estimated tax payments).

> **Example:** Jane elects to exercise and sell NSO's for 15,000 shares of NTC stock, when her exercise price is $5 per share and the market value is $100 per share. She will get gross proceeds from the sale of $1,500,000. Assuming her current year earnings are in excess of the FICA limits for Social Security taxes, she will have to give a total of $494,663 to the company when she exercises the stock ($75,000 for the exercise price, $399,000 of income tax withholding (15,000 x 95 x .28) plus $20,663 of Medicare (15,000 x 95 x .0145). She will have $1,005,337 left, at the time of exercise; however, she will have to pay another

$165,300 [(15,000 x 95 x .396)—$399,000] of income taxes, with her tax return, on April 15 of the following year).

Paying for the Shares and Taxes

You are probably thinking you should wait until your shares have a market value substantially in excess of the option price, in order to get maximum benefit from the interest free loan feature of the option. If you do, you must pay both the exercise price and the federal taxes to your company. You may not have the cash to pay for the stock, so you may make an arrangement with a brokerage firm, to which your company guarantees delivery of the option shares. You enter an order to sell the shares on the exercise date. Your company delivers the shares to your brokerage firm by the settlement date, and the brokerage firm sends the exercise price and the required tax payment to the company. The balance of the proceeds are placed in your account or delivered to you.

In some cases, your company facilitates a cashless exercise, by delivering shares that are equal to the gross market value of the option shares, less the sum of the exercise price and the required tax deposit.

In either case, you have converted your entire equity to cash, and you are free to diversify your investments or use the proceeds for other purposes.

While an exercise and sale strategy is the simplest way of dealing with your options and could be the best thing to do in some circumstances, it is not the most tax efficient.

Planned Installment Exercises and Sales for Tax Efficiency

If you have a large amount of income in one year, you are likely to find yourself in a higher tax bracket than usual. In addition, you may lose some tax benefits, such as personal exemptions and itemized deductions. The tax cost of recognizing a great deal of income in one year can be shocking.

You may benefit from exercising your options on an installment basis, over a number of years. Many times, your CPA or another tax professional must prepare pro-forma tax estimates for several years into the future, in order to understand the benefits, if any, from a strategy of installment exercises. In addition, you need to examine your stock option plan, to determine if partial exercises are permitted and the minimum exercise amount.

Opportunity to Balance and Manage Risks of Concentrated Position

An installment exercise, combined with periodic sales, can be a compromise that allows you to enjoy some of the benefits of tax deferral, from delaying the exercise of the option, while addressing critical needs or concerns. You, like most employees, probably believe in the long-term success of your employer and want retain a stake in the company's long-term growth. Where the company stock has significant value and the option has a substantial exercise price, you are wise to use the leverage, by not exercising any of your options, because the unexercised options provide a risk free, highly leveraged participation in that growth.

Installment exercises and partial sales eventually become a part of many strategies because of the inherent balance of risk, rewards and investor goals.

Postpone or Hold Full Option Term

The reasons you would postpone or hold your NSO's full term are primarily the same as discussed in Chapter Seven. You may be bullish on the stock and want to delay payment for the stock and taxes. If you hold NSO's, you must pay ordinary income tax on the bargain element when the options are exercised, and, normally, you will have to sell much more stock or accumulate substantially more cash, than the holder of ISO's. As discussed previously, this can be a risky strategy, when dealing with a large bargain element.

Exercise and Hold NSO's for Tax Efficiency

Most exercise and hold strategies are tax motivated and focus on moving as much of the gain on the options as possible, from being taxed as compensation income, at ordinary rates of up to 39.6%, to being taxed as long-term capital gains, at rates limited to a 20% maximum. In other words, you can cut the tax burden in half, by exercising and holding the stock for 12 months.

The bargain element on the exercise date is taxed as compensation at ordinary income tax rates. Any appreciation or decline in value after the exercise date is treated as capital gains or losses. Gains on shares held more than 12 months after the exercise date are taxed at the favorable rates for long-term capital gains. This advantage encourages many to exercise early, in anticipation of holding the shares for long-term appreciation.

An early exercise requires you to give up the interest-free loan feature of the option and requires you to commit personal resources to the investment risk of holding the shares. Your financial commitment is the total of the exercise price for the shares, transaction costs, and income taxes on the bargain element.

An early exercise also bears the risk of non-deductible loss, should the shares decline in value. All losses from the shares declining in value are capital losses and cannot be offset against the compensation income, which must be reported when the options are exercised, even if the shares are sold in the year of exercise. The deduction for capital losses is limited to the amount of capital gains on other transactions, plus $3,000. Any unused excess is carried forward to the next year.

> **Example:** Jane makes an early exercise of NSO's for 15,000 shares, when the market value is $10 per share and the exercise price is $5 per share. She makes a total cash investment of $105,788 (15,000 x 5 for exercise price; 15,000 x 5 x .396 for income taxes; and 15,000 x 5 x .0145 for Medicare taxes). If the company goes broke, and she has no other capital gains against which to offset her loss, she will be allowed to deduct $3,000 per year on her tax return. This deduction is worth a maximum of $1,188 per year in tax savings ($3,000 x .396). It takes a long time to recover $105,788, at the rate of $1,188 per year.

Tax Deferral Planning

Long-term deferral is a basic element of many tax-planning strategies, and should be taken into consideration when managing the tax liability attributable to NSO's. However, tax deferral can take on many different faces, depending on your long-term goals.

A simple deferral is accomplished by delaying the exercise as long as possible. This maximizes the deferral of the taxes that will be due on the bargain element of the option. However, there are no strategies for reducing the tax when the options are eventually exercised, or for deferring it beyond the expiration of the option.

In contrast, the tax on appreciation in value after the exercise date can be reduced by offsetting the gain on the option shares with capital losses from other transactions. Gains can be deferred indefinitely by holding the shares until they pass to heirs, through an estate and receive a stepped up in cost basis allowed for inherited assets. The use of strategies, such as charitable remainder trusts, can defer the taxes and permit you to redirect a portion of the taxes to a charity of your choice. You also have considerably more flexibility in your estate planning when you hold shares as compared to unexercised options. Some of these strategies are discussed later.

Finally, holding both unexercised options and company shares results in a concentrated risk for many employees. All of your investment positions should be carefully evaluated, to make certain you are taking only the risks that are necessary and appropriate to your position and long-term goals.

Chapter 9

Concentrated Stock Position Strategies

Overview

Concentrated stock positions have the potential to create great wealth. According to iQuantic, a consulting firm in San Francisco, more than $500 billion in new wealth was created via options during 1999. A large part of that wealth was in new, volatile technology companies.

Investors may be holding a highly concentrated position, for a variety of reasons.

1. Shares were received as compensation through the exercise of employee stock options.
2. A private company has a successful *Initial Public Offering*.
3. A company sells to public company in a stock-for-stock transaction.
4. A single investment appreciates dramatically.

5. Stock is received through as a gift, typically from a family member.

Diversify to Reduce Risk

Wealth is best protected and safely grown over time through diversification. We have all heard the adage, "Don't put all your eggs in one basket." This does not mean you need to cash out of a successful position and hide the cash in your mattress, but it does mean that it is wise to spread your risks among several high quality investments. Often, investors have a difficult time removing emotions and making goal driven, logical decisions about the stock that, in many cases, has made them wealthy.

> Even if you are particularly bullish on the underlying stock, it is prudent to diversify a portion of the overall position.

Example: In the early to mid-1980's, IBM seemed to be unstoppable and the stock soared, creating hundreds of millionaires in a short period of time. Many executives naively believed the exponential acceleration would never end. A large majority ignored advisors, who suggested they diversify and lock in some of their newly created wealth. Their eyes were riveted on the ever-increasing stock price. Their blind arrogance, coupled with greed, overpowered any feelings of fear, and many failed to diversify. Starting in 1987, the stock began sliding. At this point, their fear overpowered their greed, and many sold large positions that cost them thousands, some millions, of dollars. The IBM stock price sank and the price chart formed a bowl-like formation, for about 10 years.

If a prudent investor—taking minimal risks—were to have sold and diversified, earning a mere 7% a year over that ten-year period, he would have doubled his money. The IBM shareholders barely broke even over the same time period.

Strategies Based on Needs and Goals

Each investor has individual needs, objectives and desires. Investors holding concentrated positions frequently need to generate cash flow, create current liquidity, reduce risk, minimize income taxes, protect shareholder voting rights and influence, and transfer wealth to the next generation, in the most tax efficient way.

Investors usually identify with one or more of the following general goals:
- Create liquidity
- Hedge risk
- Diversify
- Transfer Wealth

Strategy Matrix

Depending on your goals, one or more strategies should be explored and a customized solution created, to best fit your particular needs. The following is a matrix of strategies that allow you to accomplish one or more of the four general investment goals.

Concentrated Stock Strategies

STRATEGIES	GOALS			
	Create Liquidity	Hedge	Diversify	Wealth Transfer
Sale on the open market	xx		xx	
Sell privately at a discount	xx		xx	
Get a loan against a position	xx			
Write covered call	xx			
Purchase put option		xx		
Monetization of protected positions	xx	xx	xx	
Zero-premium collar		xx		
Zero-premium collar with purpose loan	xx	xx	xx	
Zero-premium collar with non-purpose loan	xx	xx	xx	
Zero-premium participating collar		xx		
Sell short against the box		xx		
Exchange fund			xx	
Variable prepaid forward contract	xx	xx	xx	
Custom liquidity contract	xx	xx	xx	
Charitable gifting				xx
Charitable remainder trust				xx
Charitable lead trust				xx
Family foundation				xx

Figure 9.1

Before entering into a particular strategy it is important to first understand how the transaction fits with your overall financial condition. The best way to achieve your goals when using one of these strategies is to make sure you have a financial *super-structure* that accounts for all the different factors that are involved with your situation. This super-structure should outline your goals, objectives and considerations, and be a blueprint to coordinate the legal, tax and investment professionals guiding you.

The different strategies discussed in this section are not simple and often may be referred to differently, depending on the institution or individual describing them. Each strategy should be customized for you; therefore, the subsequent information should be viewed as informative, but not absolute. Often, an individual will enter into a combination of strategies that span several months or years to achieve a variety of objectives. Rarely, are transactions the same and often the structure of the strategy is very flexible depending upon the factors of the situation. Therefore, the strategies discussed are dynamic and like the institutions creating them, ever evolving. Hopefully, this section will help you understand the basics so you can speak intelligently about your stock, and it will help you qualify the right advisors.

Sale on the Open Market
[Goals: Liquidity, Diversification]

As we have previously stressed, you should start the management process by first defining your goals. However, the next important question you need to answer is, "How much of my wealth and financial security would I invest in this stock or position, if I were starting with cash today?" If the answer is, "A whole lot less than I currently have invested!" then you need to rearrange your portfolio.

To implement a new strategy, the outright sale of a portion of a concentrated position may be highly desirable. It is simple and eliminates all risks that are specific to the concentrated position. You have maximum flexibility to diversify your portfolio and spread your risk over a number of companies and industries. The significant disadvantages of an outright sale are a large reduction in the investment base, because of income taxes and exclusion from future appreciation in the liquidated position. In addition, sales by key executives may be perceived as a negative prediction for the future prospects of the company and put downward pressure on the stock price.

Restricted and control stock is described in Chapter Four. If you are selling control or restricted stock, you must comply with Rule 144. The amount that can be sold may be limited, and you must follow the reporting requirements of the SEC regulations.

Sell Privately at a Discount
[Goal: liquidity, Diversification]

If you are selling control or restricted stock that is not yet publicly traded, then you may have a difficult time disposing of the stock, and may have to sell it, at a discount, in a private sale, because of its lack of marketability.

Get a Loan Against a Position
[Goal: Liquidity]

If you hold restricted stock, you may be able to use the stock as collateral for a loan, in order to free up some capital. A bank or brokerage firm may hold the securities and lend a percentage of the market value, while charging interest on the amount lent to you.

Write a Covered Call
[Goal: liquidity]

You may choose to sell or write an over-the-counter covered call option, in order to enhance your yield. You receive an up-front premium payment for the sale of the covered call option, which gives the buyer of the option the right to purchase the stock at a specific price. If the stock decreases in value, the decrease will be partially offset by the premium received from the sale of the call. You can write the call amount at whatever price best meets your financial objectives. The seller of the call retains dividend income from the stock and the voting rights of the shares.

> **Example:** If you own 50,000 shares of NTC in January, when the current market value is $100 per share, you may elect to write December covered calls at $130 for a $3 premium. You will have sold someone the right to purchase your 50,000 shares, when the share price reaches $130 or better, before December. If the share price rises to $150, before expiration, the buyer of the option will exercise his option to call the shares away from you, at $130. You will receive all dividends, retain voting rights, realize 30 percent appreciation in the stock, before it is called away, and keep the $150,000 premium for the option. If the stock drops to $80, during this time, the buyer of the option will *not* exercise his option to purchase the stock at $130, and the option will expire, worthless. Your loss of $20 in share price will be partially offset by the $3 received for the option, and you would net a $17 loss, instead of a $20 loss.

NOTE: An investor who writes a covered call still has downside exposure, and is unable to participate in the appreciation of the stock over the call strike price. Normally, investors must pledge shares to the facilitating brokerage firm, as collateral, to ensure delivery, if the option is exercised. Investors holding restricted or control stock may be limited in the number of options they may write. It is important to note that over-the-counter contracts are not actively traded, and, therefore, liquidity is a concern.

Purchase a Put Option
[Goal: Hedge]

If you are interested in protecting the downside of your position, you may elect to purchase a put option on the underlying shares. This works like insurance. There is a premium paid up front, in order to protect your downside risk. By purchasing a put option, you have the right to sell the securities at a specific price per share. You know the value of the number of shares protected, for the duration of the contract.

You have wide flexibility in structuring the protective position. A full protection of the current market value may be quite expensive, while protecting 80% of the current value may be considerably less. Generally, the more volatile the stock price and the greater the percentage of the market value protected, the higher the premium required to purchase the options.

You have the advantage of participating in the full amount of all future appreciation, and may be able to borrow a substantial portion of the portfolio value, by posting the protected shares as collateral.

> **Example:** You have 60,000 shares of NTC and the market price per share is $100, in January. Your cost per share is $25, so your unrealized gain is $75 ($100 less $25). You hope the stock will continue to appreciate, but you're afraid that the price will drop, and you are at risk of losing up to $6,000,000 dollars. To protect your downside and still participate in the potential upside, you purchase a put option. You buy a December $90 put option at $3 a share. This means you have the right to sell your shares, for a minimum of $90, until the contract expires in December. If the share price continues to appreciate to $150, the contract will

expire and be worthless, and you will have lost $3 a share or $180,000 ($3 x 60,000 shares). On the other hand, if the stock price falls to $60, you can elect to exercise the contract and sell your shares at $90. You will receive a total of $5,400,000 from the sale of the stock (60,000 x $90). The protective put strategy will have given you a benefit of $1,620,000, the difference between the market price and the option price, minus the $3 put premium ($27 x 60,000 shares). **A net gain of $1,620,000.**

If you have held the shares for more than 12 months, before hedging your position, the purchase of the put will not have an effect on your holding period for tax purposes. However, the holding period of the shares will be terminated if you have held them for less than 12 months. If your holding period for a block of shares is terminated, a new holding period will begin on the day after the put is sold or expires. You are not allowed to deduct the cost of the put contracts, if it expires or is sold for a loss. The cost or loss is added to your cost basis for the shares.

Though this is a good way to hedge price risk, it requires you to pay the premium up front. You receive dividend income and retain your voting rights while participating in the hedge.

While a put can give predictable protection at the end of the contract period, it may not fully protect you against price fluctuations during the term of the contract, and, as a result, you may have to retain the position until the end of the contract to get the full benefit of the hedge position. As a put nears expiration, it may become illiquid, making it particularly difficult to manage for unexpected contingencies.

Finally, you must be careful not to run afoul of the security regulations, particularly Section 16(b) restricting short swing profits and the prohibitions against using insider information.

Example of Purchasing a Put Option

EXAMPLE OF PURCHASING A PUT OPTION	
Security position	60,000 shares of New Tech Co
Market price at beginning	$100 per share
Market value of portfolio	$6,000,000
Hedging strategy	Purchase of put options to protect the investor's entire position at $90 per share for one year; put premium of $3.00 per share
Initial cost	$180,000
PORTFOLIO VALUE AFTER ONE YEAR WITH FALLING STOCK PRICE	
Market price after one year	$60 per share
Portfolio value	Market value of shares 3,600,000 Intrinsic value of put options 1,800,000 Total 5,400,000
PORTFOLIO VALUE AFTER ONE YEAR WITH RISING STOCK PRICE	
Market price after one year	$130 per share
Portfolio value	Market value of shares 7,800,000 Less option cost (180,000) 7,620,000

Figure 9.2

Monetization of Protected Positions
[Goals: Liquidity, Hedge, Diversification]

An equity position, protected by a put option, becomes very secure collateral that can be used to secure a term loan.

Customarily, a brokerage firm will be willing to lend you 90% to 95% of the market value protected by the put options. The brokerage firm requires periodic payment of the interest during the term of the loan.

Federal Reserve Regulations limit the amount of the loan to 50% of the market value, if loan proceeds are used to invest in equity securities (shares of other companies). These are called *purpose loans. Non-purpose loans* can be used to invest in fixed income securities, or for other purposes, and may be for the full 90% to 95% of the protected value.

> **Example:** You may own 60,000 shares, having a market price of $100 per share. The market value is $6,000,000. If you purchase put protection at $90 per share, the protected value is $5,400,000. You can get a non-purpose loan of $4,860,000 ($5,400,000 x 90%) or a purpose loan of $3,000,000 ($6,000,000 x 50%).

There is no taxable event when you purchase the put or obtain the loan. However, the combination of the long stock position and the put option is likely to be a straddle for tax purposes. If the combination is a straddle, any losses on the put option are deferred and offset against gains on the underlying stock position at the time the shares are sold. Any profits from the put option are taxed as short-term capital gains if the put position is closed in a cash settlement.

Your holding period for stock held less than 12 months will be terminated on the date a protective put is purchased, regardless of whether the put creates a straddle. The holding period begins anew on the day after the put expires or is sold. The holding period of shares held more than 12 months is not affected by a protective put position.

The rules regarding taxation of investment income from investing the loan proceeds, deducting the interest on the loan, identifying shares protected by put positions, and related tax issues are complex, sometimes ambiguous, and frequently based on the specific circumstances of a particular investor. Further, equity hedging transactions are subject to complex banking and securities regulations. As an investor, you should obtain personal tax and legal advice, to make certain you understand the tax affects and your regulatory obligations, when participating in a particular strategy.

PROFILE OF MONETIZING A PROTECTED PUT POSITION

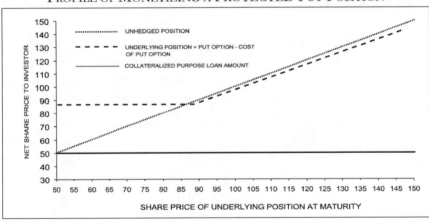

Figure 9.3

Zero-Premium Collar Strategy
[Goal: Hedge]

You may like the idea of having the downside protection that a put provides, yet, may lack the liquidity or be unwilling to pay the premium for the protection. In this case, you may employ a zero-premium collar strategy. With this strategy, you purchase a put option to hedge the price risk, and then sell a covered call option out of the money against the underlying shares, in order to achieve a net zero premium. You have the flexibility of some downside protection and some participation in the upside appreciation. How much you can lose or profit on the position lies within the spread between the put and the call.

Equity options can be customized for you, by adjusting the time horizon, the level of protection, and the degree to which you participate in future appreciation of the underlying stock position.

> **Example:** You have 60,000 shares of NTC, trading at $100 per share. You are interested in protecting your downside, but are unwilling to pay the premium of $3 per share, $180,000, for the put option contract. So, you decide to participate in a zero-premium collar. You decide to buy a December $90 put option (the right to sell) at $3 per share and to sell a December 120 covered call option at $3. This way, you do not have to come up with the cash to pay for the put premium, and your position is hedged.
>
> If the price per share falls to $75, you have the right, through your put option, to sell your shares at $90, thus protecting your downside risk.

If the price per share increases to $130, the shares will be called away from you, at $120, by the owner of the call option, leaving you with participation in the first 20% appreciation of the stock. Therefore, your downside is protected and you are able to participate in a specific amount of appreciation in the stock.

If the stock trades within the $90 to $120 range, both the put and call contract will expire and be worthless.

You must take great care to avoid a constructive sale, by simultaneously purchasing and selling a combination of puts and calls that are too close to the market price. The tax laws are ambiguous as to exactly what is permitted. However, as a practical matter, the general consensus is that a typical collar spread that is at least 10% above and below the market price will not be considered a constructive sale.

The combination of a collar and a long position in the underlying stock may be considered a straddle for tax purposes. The tax treatment of straddles and the other tax considerations regarding holding periods and interest on loans are discussed in Chapter Five.

You must pledge eligible shares as collateral to the facilitating brokerage firm. Over-the-counter contracts are not liquid, and as options near expirations, you may not be able to unwind the transaction.

If you have control stock, you can run afoul of Section 16(b) restrictions, on short-term profits and should be aware of Rule 144 limitations, on the sale of restricted or control shares and other securities law regulations.

Example of a Zero-Premium Collar

EXAMPLE OF A ZERO-PREMIUM COLLAR	
Security position	60,000 shares of New Tech Co
Market price at beginning	$100 per share
Market value of portfolio	$6,000,000
Hedging strategy	Purchase of put options to protect the investor's entire position at $90 per share for one year; put premium of $3.00 per share
	Sell call options on investor's entire position at a strike price of $120 for $3.00 per share
	Put premium paid with proceeds from sale of call
Initial cost	Zero
PORTFOLIO VALUE AFTER ONE YEAR WITH FALLING STOCK PRICE	
Market price after one year	$75 per share
Portfolio value	Market value of shares 4,500,000 Intrinsic value of put options 900,000 Net value 5,400,000
PORTFOLIO VALUE AFTER ONE YEAR WITH RISING STOCK PRICE	
Market price after one year	$130 per share
Portfolio value	Market value of shares 7,800,000 Less intrinsic value of call (600,000) Net value 7,200,000
PORTFOLIO VALUE AFTER ONE YEAR WITH MODERATE PRICE INCREASE	
Market price after one year	$110 per share
Portfolio value	Market value of shares 6,600,000 Less intrinsic value of calls/puts 0 Net value 6,600,000

Figure 9.4

Zero-premium Collar with Purpose and Non-purpose Loans
[Goals: Liquidity, hedge, diversification]

The put side of the collar creates the same protected collateral position described in the preceding chapter, and you can borrow money, to build a secondary diversified position or obtain cash for other purposes. All of the limitations and other considerations discussed, with regard to loans secured by protected collateral positions, are applicable to collared positions.

PROFILE OF MONETIZING A ZERO-PREMIUM COLLAR

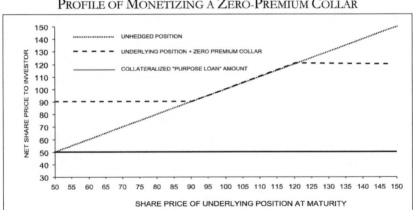

Figure 9.5

Zero-premium Participating Collar
[Goal: Hedge]

If you believe your stock will continue to appreciate, but you're not sure that you are willing to risk losing what you could realize immediately, by selling the position, you may wish to participate in a zero-premium participating collar, which will provide downside protection without giving up all potential appreciation above a strike price.

In this strategy, you would purchase a put option on the entire amount, to limit the securities downside, but would sell calls on only enough of the shares to offset the cost of the put. This way, you could participate in the appreciation of the shares that are not covered by call options. The strike price on the calls would be closer to the current market price of the shares than in a normal or straight collar. Therefore, the shares that you wrote calls on are more likely to be called away because the strike price is lower.

> **Example:** You have 60,000 shares, trading at $100, and you are having a difficult time sleeping at night, because you're worried the stock will drop and significantly affect your net worth. Yet, you still believe in your company and do not want to give up all participation if the stock were to double or even triple. You want the protection, but are unable to come up with $180,000 for the put option premium. So, you elect to structure a zero-premium participating collar. You purchase a December 90 put option on 60,000 shares, at $3 a share, and, simultaneously, write or sell a December 110 call option, on 48,000 shares, for $3.75 a share. The premiums paid and received offset each other, leaving you protected and participating at no cost. If the stock drops to $75 a share, you will be

protected and have the right to sell the securities for $90 a share. On the other hand, if the shares appreciate to $125 per share, 48,000 shares will be called away from you, and you will realize 10% more than if you would have sold at $100 per share. Your put options will expire and be worthless, and the 12,000 shares that you keep will be worth an additional 25% more, giving you room to reevaluate your situation.

A zero-premium participating collar is a strategy suitable for you if you're interested in protecting your downside, while retaining participation in the future appreciation of the un-collared portion of your shares. You retain dividend and voting rights on all shares, during the term of the contract.

Currently, collars are not considered constructive sales, as long as the difference between the put strike price and the call strike price is at least 20%, but a collar may be considered a straddle. Internal Revenue Code Sections 263(g), 1092, 1234A and 1256 provide the tax straddle rules. A detailed explanation of the rules and related legal authorities is beyond the scope of this book. You should seek out qualified legal and tax advice.

Example of a Zero-Premium Participating Collar

EXAMPLE OF A ZERO-PREMIUM PARTICIPATING COLLAR	
Security position	60,000 shares of New Tech Co
Market price at beginning	$100 per share
Market value of portfolio	$6,000,000
Hedging strategy	Purchase of put options to protect the investor's entire position at $90 per share for one year; put premium of $3 per share
	Sell call options on 80% of investor's position at a strike price of $110 for $3.75 per share
	Put premium paid with proceeds from sale of call
Initial cost	Zero
PORTFOLIO VALUE AFTER ONE YEAR WITH FALLING STOCK PRICE	
Market price after one year	$75 per share
Portfolio value	Market value of shares 4,500,000 Intrinsic value of put options 900,000 Net value 5,400,000
PORTFOLIO VALUE AFTER ONE YEAR WITH RISING STOCK PRICE	
Market price after one year	$125 per share
Portfolio value	Market value of shares 7,500,000 Less intrinsic value of call (720,000) Net value 6,780,000
PORTFOLIO VALUE AFTER ONE YEAR WITH MODERATE PRICE INCREASE	
Market price after one year	$105 per share
Portfolio value	Market value of shares 6,300,000 Less intrinsic value of calls/puts 0 Net value 6,300,000

Figure 9.6

PROFILE OF MONETIZING A ZERO-PREMIUM PARTICIPATING COLLAR

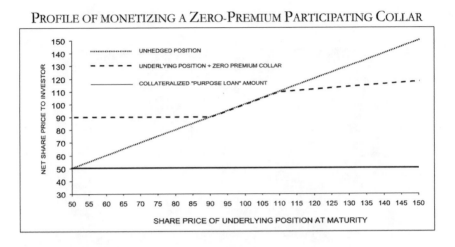

Figure 9.7

Sell Short-Against-the-Box
[Goal: Hedge]

If you are long in stock, acquired from a NSO (*not* an ISO or an ESPP held less than the 24 month or 12 month minimum periods), you may choose to short the stock or go short-against-the-box in order to protect your gain and temporarily defer taxes.

When you "short" a stock, you profit when the stock falls in value. In a short sale, you borrow stock from someone who is long or owns it, and then you sell the borrowed stock. You hope the share price will decrease, so that you can purchase the shares at a lower price and return the original number of shares back to the person who lent the stock. You profit by the difference between the share sale price and the share purchase price.

In a short-against-the-box transaction, you deposit the long shares in a custodial account (the box) with a brokerage or counter-party bank. Then, the brokerage or bank borrows the same number of shares and sells the borrowed shares in the market. So, if you are both long and short in the same stock, you are tightly hedged, or neutral.

> **Example:** If you are long 50,000 shares of NTC, trading at $100, and would like to protect your gain, you may sell short-against-the-box. This strategy will allow you to lock in 50,000 shares at $100. If the share price of NTC appreciates to $200 a share, your short position will offset the long, and you will have no additional benefit. If the share price of NTC falls to $50 per share, you are protected by gains on the short position. You are neutral and can eventually close the position by using your long shares to repay the borrowed stock.

The Tax Reform Act of 1997 lists short-against-the-box transactions as constructive sales, if the position is not closed out thirty-days after the end of the tax year in which the transaction was structured (typically January 30th). Further, you are prohibited from entering another short position or from buying put options on identical stock for 60 days after closing the short position. Re-establishing a short position within 60 days, or purchasing put options within 60 days will allow the IRS to tax you as if you sold the stock on the initial short date.

The holding period of a stock is terminated while there is an open short position and does not resume until the position is closed out. This can substantially postpone the time at which a position qualifies for long-term capital gains treatment. A short sale strategy should not be used for ISO stock or ESPP stock that has not fulfilled their holding periods, because it may be viewed by the IRS as a disqualifying disposition, and the participants will have to report compensation income. If the stock is long-term before the transaction, it will remain long-term, but short-term losses in the short position may be viewed as long-term losses. If heirs inherit a position arranged in a short-against-the-box strategy, they will not receive a step-up in the tax basis, and a capital gains tax will be charged on the profit, when the shares are eventually sold or used to close the short position.

Participate in an Exchange Fund
[Goal: Diversification]

Diversification is the traditional cornerstone of wealth protection. An exchange fund is a tax efficient means of diversifying highly concentrated, low basis positions without paying a capital gains tax. You are usually required to have a minimum of $1 million of stock in the underlying publicly traded company, and more than $5 million in other liquid investments. Exchange funds are private placements facilitated by large resourceful financial institutions, and are exempt from registration under the Securities Act of 1933. The goal of the fund is to provide diversification while deferring taxes.

The fund has a manager who selects qualified participants to contribute a portion of their highly appreciated stock. The contributions then represent a diversified basket of securities. All securities enter a basket—a fund that is organized as a limited partnership—and each investor gets a proportionate partnership interest that is based on the market value of the securities he contributes. If you participate as an investor, you are allowed to withdraw your proportionate share of the partnership portfolio after seven years by taking a number of different stocks. Effectively, you have converted your investment in one stock into an investment in a number of high quality stocks, to diversify your portfolio, all *on a tax free basis.* The new stocks still have the low basis of the old stock that was contributed to the partnership, and capital gains taxes will be charged if the new stocks are sold.

Because an exchange fund is organized as a limited partnership, the fund follows Sub-chapter K of the Internal Revenue Code. The rules in Section 721 of the Internal Revenue Code allow contributions to the fund to classified as non-taxable events. Distributions of the original shares back to the original investor during the first seven years following his contribution may require the investor to recognize a portion of the unrealized gain on the contributed stock. After seven years, the fund manager may select securities to be distributed to the investor as redemption of his interest in the partnership.

> **Example:** You exchange five million dollars worth of low basis New Tech Company stock for an interest in a fund made up of a number of other stocks. The transfer of the stock to the fund is not considered a taxable event, and you will have diversified your holdings by converting your investment in a single stock into an investment in the diversified portfolio held by the fund. You will have accomplished this without paying any taxes. Your non-systematic (company-specific) risk has been substantially eliminated, and you continue to benefit from an investment in quality stocks that can be expected to appreciate at least as fast as the general market. After the required participation time, a basket of diversified stocks, that might include investments in company such as Walmart, Texaco, General Electric, and Pfizer, can be distributed tax-free to you to replace your previous concentrated investment in New Tech Company.

Exchange funds may accept restricted securities, and by so doing, allow you an opportunity to reduce risk without selling in the open market.

This may be attractive if you are an insider and fear that selling large number of shares will adversely affect the market price of your stock. Participation in an exchange fund is not considered a public sale. Therefore, a control person may be able to transfer more shares than can be sold under Rule 144, but if you are subject to Section 16(b), you need to file Form 4, and should consult with a qualified attorney about Schedule 13D and Schedule 13G filings. Exchange funds may be used as an estate planning tool, because your partnership interest, and the shares distributed in redemption of the partnership interest receive a step up in tax basis at your death. An exchange fund can be a good strategy for holders of highly appreciated stock, whose objectives are to diversify and defer taxes.

Example of an Exchange Fund

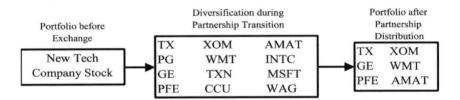

Figure 9.8

Variable Pre-paid Forward Contracts
[Goals: Liquidity, Diversification]

If you want to receive a cash advance for the majority of a concentrated position, rather than the normal 50% made available for purpose loans on put protected positions, you may choose to participate in a variable pre-paid forward contract. A forward contract works much like a collar, having both a floor and a cap price. In this contractual strategy, you agree to deliver some or all of your stock to the lender on a future date in exchange for an immediate cash payment. The cash paid to you represents a discounted forward sale price for the shares of stock, normally 75% to 90% of a protected market price. Most banks and brokerages are limited, under normal lending rules, to 50% of the market value of a position, even if the position is protected by put option contracts. The current view is that general margin restrictions do not apply to variable pre-paid forward contracts. Forward contracts have not been addressed under margin rule restrictions. Therefore, you are given the full cash advance, even if the proceeds are to be invested in the stock market.

In a variable pre-paid forward contract, the number of shares you must deliver to repay the advance varies based upon the value of the stock when the contract matures. If the stock appreciates, you deliver only enough shares to repay the original cash advance, plus an increase to compensate for the time that has expired during the term of the contract. The price used to compute the number of shares necessary to satisfy your obligation is capped, as in the case of a zero-premium collar. If the value of the stock decreases below a predetermined level, your obligation is limited to delivering all of the stock committed to the contract. The contract guarantees you a minimum sales price (the amount of your advance) and provides immediate cash. If the shares appreciate in value, you fully participate in the growth, up to cap price set by the contract. Upfront, you receive a discounted amount where the interest charge for the amount lent is pre-paid.

The contract is customized to meet your individual objectives. The floor can be set at a percentage that you are comfortable with, and the upper cap is adjusted accordingly.

Example: You own 60,000 shares of NTC, with a current market price of $100 per share and want to convert a majority of your position into a diversified portfolio of equities. You may enter into a two-year pre-paid forward contract and obtain a cash advance equal to 75% of the current market value, $4,500,000 (60,000 shares x $100 x 75%). Your floor price would be set $90 (90%) and a cap price set at $144 (144%).

You can invest the $4,500,000, wherever you see fit, including a diversified equity portfolio. Your contract allows you to fully participate in all appreciation, up to $144 per share. If your contract is based on a protected value of $90 per share and your obligation is limited to delivering the 60,000 shares at the end of the contract, you are effectively guaranteed a sale price of $90 per share. Even if the market price falls to $50 per share, you are only obligated to deliver the 60,000 shares. Your loss is limited. You effectively lock in the $90 per share at the beginning of the contract, and the financial institution most likely will use some form of hedging strategy to protect it against market declines.

Example of a Variable Pre-paid Forward Contract

EXAMPLE OF A PREPAID FORWARD CONTRACT	
Security position	60,000 shares of New Tech Co
Market price at beginning	$100 per share
Market value of portfolio	$6,000,000
Hedging strategy	Prepaid contract that provides 90% downside protection below current price. Investor participates in first 44% of appreciation.
	No call or put premiums paid
	Cash advance to investor for 75% of protected value (the present value of current share price due in two years): the investor is required to repay 100% of the protected value or deliver 100% of the position if the share price is below $90 Cash advance of $4,500,000
Term	2 years
PORTFOLIO VALUE AFTER TWO YEARS WITH FALLING STOCK PRICE	
Market price after two years	$50 per share
Results	Portfolio has value of $3,000,000 ($50 x 60,000)
	Investor delivers all of the shares (60,000) and keeps the $4,500,000 advanced at the beginning of the contract; net benefit of **$1,500,000**
PORTFOLIO VALUE AFTER TWO YEARS WITH MODERATE PRICE INCREASE	
Market price after two year	$110
Results	Portfolio value: $110 x 60,000 = $6,600,000
	Investor delivers 49,091 shares; Investor keeps the $4,500,000 initial cash advance plus 10,909 shares of stock (10,909 x $110 = $1,200,000) for a total value of **$5,700,000** ($6,600,000 less interest for two years)
PORTFOLIO VALUE AFTER TWO YEARS WITH SUBSTANTIAL PRICE INCREASE	
Market price after two year	$155
Results	Portfolio value: $155 x 60,000 = $9,300,000
	Investor delivers 39,096 shares. Investor keeps the $4,500,000 initial cash advance plus 20,904 shares of stock (20,904 x $155 = $3,250,000) for a total value of **$7,740,000** ($8,640,000 less interest for two years)

Figure 9.9

A variable pre-paid forward contract allows you to protect your concentrated position and frees up a majority of your value to be allocated to other investments. This flexibility enables you to reduce your risks, yet continue to participate in the growth of the stock. You are also able to reinvest the proceeds to grow your portfolio.

A variable pre-paid forward contract allows you to retain voting and dividend rights. They normally are not treated as a constructive sale for tax purposes, but are considered tax straddles.

The method of settling pre-paid forward contracts affects how they are taxed. If you settle the contract by delivering the stock (as compared with making a cash payment), you will be taxed on the basis of a completed sale of the stock. The difference between your basis and the cash advance will be included in your income as a capital gain. If the stock is below the floor when settled, you report a gain as if you sold the stock for the loan proceeds.

Some pre-paid forwards may allow you to participate in a percentage of growth over the cap price. Again, a combination of strategies may be utilized to accomplish your individual goals.

Custom Liquidity Contracts
[Goals: Liquidity, Diversification]

A customized liquidity contract is similar to a pre-paid forward contract, but is settled in cash rather than with actual stocks. Using the same example as above and settling the contract with cash, instead of delivering shares, you can see that both transactions protect you on the downside and give you participation on the upside. In this example, you receive the same floor set at 90% and cap set at 144%. An actual contract would reflect many factors; hopefully, the table below will help you understand the basic concept.

Example of a Customized Liquidity Contract

EXAMPLE OF A CUSTOMIZED LIQUIDITY CONTRACT	
Security position	60,000 shares of New Tech Co
Market price at beginning	$100 per share
Market value of portfolio	$6,000,000
Hedging strategy	Liquidity contract that provides 90% downside protection below current price. Investor participates in first 44% of appreciation.
	No call or put premiums paid
	Cash advance to investor for 75% of market value
	Reference Price (floor) of $90
	Cap Price of $144
	Cash advance of $4,500,000
Term	2 years
PORTFOLIO VALUE AFTER TWO YEARS WITH FALLING STOCK PRICE	
Market price after two years	$50 per share
Results	Investor pays financial institution the value of the position: 60,000 x $50 per share, a total of $3,000,000, versus stock worth $3,000,000
Benefits	Immediate cash liquidity and protection against decline of stock value below Reference Price (60,000 x ($90 - $50 = **$2,400,000** of value), Value includes prepaid interest for two years.
PORTFOLIO VALUE AFTER TWO YEARS WITH MODERATE PRICE INCREASE	
Market price after two years	$110
Results	Investor pays financial institution the the reference price per share: 60,000 x $90, a total of $5,400,000, versus stock worth $6,600,000.
Benefits	Immediate cash liquidity, protection against possible price declines and participation in stock appreciation above Reference Price (60,000 x ($110 - $90) = **$1,200,000** of value)
PORTFOLIO VALUE AFTER TWO YEARS WITH SUBSTANTIAL PRICE INCREASE	
Market price after two years	$155
Results	The investor pays the financial institution the Reference Price plus the market price above the Cap Price: 60,000 x ($90 + ($155 - $144)), a total of $6,060,000, versus stock worth $9,300,000
Benefits	Immediate cash liquidity, protection against possible price declines and participation in stock price appreciation above Reference Price, up to the Cap Price:(60,000 x ($144 - $90) = **$3,240,000** of value)

Figure 9.10

The benefits derived from a contact that protects your downside risks are very valuable because you are able to lock in your gains over the set floor value and diversify your proceeds.

Since you are closing a straddle, the tax treatment depends on whether the underlying stock price increases or decreases during the term of the contract. The complex rules governing taxation of straddle positions are beyond the scope of this book, and the advice and guidance of skilled tax professionals is essential if you are using any strategy taxed as a straddle.

Charitable Gifting
[Goal: Wealth transfer]

If you want to make gifts to a church, your alma mater, the Red Cross, or any other charitable organization, you may want to use low basis shares from a concentrated stock position held more than 12 months (*the deduction for stock held less than 12 months is limited to the cost basis*) rather than cash to make the contribution. The charity gets the same amount of money, because it does not pay tax when it sells the stock. You get the same tax deduction (limited to 30% of your adjusted gross income), but do not include any of the gain that would be recognized if the stock were sold in order to raise cash for the contribution.

Charitable Remainder Trust
[Goal: Wealth transfer]

If you have highly appreciated stock, you may elect to gift a portion to a charitable remainder trust. If you choose to participate, you receive a current income tax deduction for a portion of assets transferred to the trust, and an ongoing income stream for the remainder of your life, or a specified number of years. Upon transfer, you reduce your taxable estate and future tax liability, and the trust is able to sell the securities without paying any capital gains tax. The full value of the investment position is retained, thus increasing the income stream that is produced by reinvesting the sale proceeds in a diversified portfolio. The portfolio grows tax-free during your life and a specified percentage of the portfolio value is distributed to you each year. The net effect is to substantially increase the income stream during your life. The trust principle goes to a designated charity or a family foundation when you die, and not to your heirs. In some cases, you can elect to hold a life insurance policy in an irrevocable life insurance trust to replace the value transferred to the charity.

> **Example:** You have 50,000 shares of NTC, trading at $200 dollars a share. After doing a very thorough analysis with your financial advisor, you realize you will never need the majority of your assets to meet your financial goals. If you do nothing, the government will continue to tax you, upon your death, at a rate of up to 55% of your total estate. So, you decide to transfer 25,000 shares to a charitable remainder trust, to benefit the disabled in your hometown.

> When the assets are transferred into the trust, you receive a charitable deduction for a portion of the fair market value. You can then sell the stock without incurring any income taxes. Instead of netting 60% to 80% after taxes, the entire proceeds can be invested in a less risky, more diversified portfolio. You can receive an enhanced income stream for the rest of your life, and after your death, the trust principal will go to supporting the social cause you selected.

A charitable remainder unitrust trust (a CRUT) is structured as an irrevocable trust, which means that once it is set up it cannot be shut down or revoked. After reviewing your goals and objectives, a charitable remainder trust may be a good vehicle to achieve a philanthropic goal and to provide enhanced cash flow. In some cases, the cash flow from the trust can be reinvested, for you to accumulate a larger investment portfolio over time than can be accumulated with the same investment strategy outside the CRT. In essence, both you and the charity enjoy financial benefits at the expense of the federal tax system.

Charitable Lead Trust
[Goal: Wealth transfer]

A charitable lead trust can be very flexible. You gift securities to a trustee of your choice. The trustee manages the trust's assets and distributes fixed dollar amount, or a specified percentage of the trust assets, to a charity, each year, for a specific number of years, or for one or more life-times. The annual gift to the charity qualifies for a federal gift tax deduction, and the trust will last for a specified time. The valuation of the future transfer of trust principle to non-charitable beneficiaries is heavily discounted, and the gift tax on the eventual transfer is mini-mized, even though it is due, when the trust is initially funded. At expiration of the trust, the non-charitable beneficiaries will receive the assets without paying any gift or estate tax. A major benefit of a charitable lead trust is that you are able to participate in the gifting of your assets during your lifetime, as opposed to after death, as is true with a charitable remainder trust.

> **Example:** You have 50,000 shares of NTC, trading at a market value of $200, and you set up a charitable lead trust for 25,000

shares. The trust begins to distribute the first of 20 fixed annual payments of $500,000 to the charity of your choice. In this case, your community is building a food bank for the needy and for victims of natural disasters. You are able to participate and derive satisfaction from the difference your contribution will make for your community. At the end of the 20 years, the assets from the trust, and all appreciation will be transferred to the designated beneficiaries, such as your two daughters, with no gift or estate tax.

A charitable lead trust is set up as an irrevocable trust and, generally, will restrict a grantor from receiving any income from the assets held by the trust.

Family Foundation
[Goal: Wealth transfer]

Usually, a family foundation is funded from your family assets and supports philanthropic causes. The funding can be made during your lifetime, from your estate, or as the remainder beneficiary of a charitable remainder trust. The assets in the trust are solely dedicated to charitable uses; the assets cannot be used to benefit your family. However, your family appoints board members to manage the investment portfolio and to control the charitable distributions. The foundation is required to distribute only five percent of its assets to charities each year. Income and profits of the family foundation are subject only to a 1% or 2% tax income tax, since the entire portfolio is dedicated to supporting qualified charitable causes.

The family foundation can be run by a self-perpetuating board and serve as a permanent legacy to the community. Management of the foundation requires the establishing of investment policies and the making of grant decisions. You may find that a family foundation supports a forum for perpetuating your family's values and encouraging participation in worthwhile organizations. The ability to provide support for worthwhile causes beyond your life can be especially appealing.

> **Example:** Jeff, an entrepreneur in Austin, literally went from rags to riches. When he began his software firm, he was living off his wife's salary and using personal savings and credit cards to fund his new venture. After three years of hard work, it paid off, and he sold his ownership in his company for more than a hundred million dollars in stock of an established, public company.
>
> Jeff's main goal, when he started his successful business, was to make a few million dollars, so he and his family could live comfortably. After the sale, he was worth more than a hundred million dollars, and obviously, it was time for him and his wife to re-evaluate their true goals and objectives. Their situation had changed drastically. Getting rich was no longer the goal, but staying that way and protecting what they had been blessed with was their main concern. They realized that they would never spend all of their wealth, and that Uncle Sam would take up to 55% in estate taxes—more than fifty million dollars—if they did not include an appropriate estate tax strategy in their plan to accomplish their family goals.
>
> After some thought, they identified certain goals that were especially important to them. For instance, they wanted to provide financial security for their five children and their

future grandchildren, so they set up appropriate trusts and education accounts. Their family had been affected by cancer, and they both had a desire to support the National Cancer Society in its search for a cure and other worthy causes, so they set up a charitable remainder trust where the remainder of the assets will be distributed to a family foundation run by their children. They also were very active in their local church and wanted to use some of their wealth for the building of a shelter for battered women and homeless children, so Jeff and his wife made a sizable gift of stock to help with the project, and had the satisfaction of seeing, first hand, what a difference their money was making in the lives of others.

As you can see, there are many strategies that can be used as tools to accomplish your goals. Some strategies are particularly useful, if you have a concentrated stock position.

Because emotions often blur the visions of investors, it is imperative that you start with very clear and refined goals. By starting with the desired end result in mind, you can work with qualified advisors, to create a strategy that is right for you.

Chapter 10

Conclusion

Our country is experiencing one of the most prosperous eras ever realized in civilization. People, from all walks of life, are taking part in the American dream. Enormous wealth is being created, in very short time, by individuals who are being rewarded for their knowledge, innovation, and hard work. Ownership, which was once hoarded by founders and key executives, is now being shared throughout the corporate structure. Employees, like you, are benefiting from stock option grants that allow participation of corporate growth and success, without requiring an outlay of cash.

You may be struggling with two very strong emotions—fear and greed. As with every boom, many of you get rich, but few of you stay that way. As we have discussed, taxes and the threat of falling stock prices can cost you all or most of your wealth. Be SMART and *protect yourself.*

When managing millions of dollars, you should realize you cannot afford to go without qualified advisors. You need professional guidance, to sort through the mound of details that can potentially save you thousands to millions of dollars. Most people get rich only once in a lifetime. There is no excuse for squandering the opportunity, by making a million dollar mistake, because you fail to formulate a plan or to seek advice.

It is our hope that this book has served as an informative guide, to help both you and your advisors develop the strategies that you need to preserve and grow your wealth intelligently.

About the Authors

Nathan Reneau and Travis Knapp are registered investment advisors at a leading global investment firm in Austin, Texas. Nathan and Travis work in a team of specialists handing all aspects of asset management for affluent investors, specializing in advising business owners and highly compensated executives on complex issues.

Travis Knapp holds a Bachelor of Business Administration, in Finance, from Mays College of Business at Texas A&M University. He specializes in equity selection, sector rotation, asset allocation and economic theory.

Nathan Reneau is a Certified Financial Planner, Certified Public Account, and a tax attorney. Nathan holds a Bachelor of Business Administration in accounting and a Jurist Doctorate from the University of Texas Law School. He has more than 20 years of experience in helping affluent families manage their wealth. Nathan also is a member of the American Institute of Certified Public Accountants, Texas Society of Certified Public Accounts, Central Texas Estate Planning Council, and Texas Bar Association.

Appendix

Sample of Typical Option Agreement

ABC Corporation 1995 Stock Option Plan

THIS AGREEMENT, made this____day of_____, 2000, by and between ABC CORPORATION, a Texas corporation (hereafter called the "Company"), and_____(hereafter called "Optionee"),

WITNESSETH THAT:

WHEREAS, the Board of Directors of the Company ("Board of Directors") has adopted the ABC Corporation 1995 Stock Option Plan (the "Plan") pursuant to which options covering an aggregate of 700,000 shares of the Common Stock of the Company may be granted to officers and other key management employees of the Company and its subsidiaries; and

WHEREAS, Optionee is now an officer or other key management employee of the Company or a subsidiary of the Company; and

WHEREAS, the Company desires to grant to Optionee the option to purchase certain shares of its stock under terms of the Plan;

NOW, THEREFORE, in consideration of the premises, and of the mutual agreements hereinafter set forth, it is covenanted and agreed as follows:

1. Grant Subject to Plan. This option is granted under and is expressly subject to, all the terms and provisions of the Plan, which terms are incorporated herein by reference. The Committee referred to in Paragraph 4 of the Plan ("Committee") has been appointed by the Board of Directors, and designated by it, as the Committee to make grants of options.

2. and Terms of Option. Pursuant to action of the Committee, which action was taken on_____("Date of Grant"), the Company grants to Optionee the option to purchase all or any part of_____(number) shares of the Common Stock of the Company, of the par value of $0.01 per share ("Common Stock"), for a period of ten (10) years from the grant date, at the purchase price of $_____per share; provided, however, that the right to exercise such option shall be, and is hereby, restricted so that no shares may be purchased during the first year of the term hereof; that at any time during the term of this option after the end of the first year from the Date of Grant, Optionee may purchase up to 33–1/3% of the total number of shares to which this option relates; that at any time during the term of this option after the end of the second year form the Date of Grant, Optionee may purchase up to an additional 33–1/3% of the total number of shares to which this option relates; so that upon the expiration of the third year from the Date of Grant and thereafter during the term hereof, Optionee will have become entitled to purchase the entire number of shares to which this option relates. In no event may this option or any part thereof be exercised after the expiration of ten (10) years form the Date of Grant. The purchase price of the shares subject to the option may be paid for (a) in cash, (b) in the discretion of the Committee, by tender of shares of Common Stock already owned by Optionee, or (c) in the discretion of the Committee, by a combination of methods of payment specified in clauses (a) and (b), all in accordance with Paragraph 8 of the Plan. No shares of Common Stock may be tendered in exercise of this option if such shares were acquired by optionee through the exercise of an Incentive Stock Option, unless (a) such shares have been held by Optionee for at least one year, and (b) at least two years have elapsed since Incentive Stock Option was granted.

3. Anti-Dilution Provisions. In the event that, during the term of this Agreement, there is any change in the number of shares of outstanding Common Stock of the Company by reason of stock dividends, recapitalizations, mergers, consolidations, split-ups, combinations or exchanges of shares and the like, the number of shares covered by this option agreement and the price thereof shall be adjusted, to the same proportionate number of shares and price as in this original agreement.

4. Investment Purpose. Optionee represents that, in the event of the exercise by him of the option hereby granted, or any part thereof, he intends to purchase the shares acquired on such exercise for investment and not with a view to resale or other distribution; except that the Company, at its election, may waive or release this condition in the event the shares acquired on exercise of the option are registered under the Securities Act of 1933, or upon the happening of any other contingency which the Company shall determine warrants the waiver or release of this condition. Optionee agrees that the certificates evidencing the shares acquired by him on exercise of all or any part of the option, may bear a restrictive legend, if appropriate, indicating that the shares have not been registered under said Act and are subject to restrictions on the transfer thereof, which legend may be in the following form (or such other form as the Company shall determine to be proper), to-wit:

"The shares represented by this certificate have not been registered under the Securities Act of 1933, but have been issues of transferred to the registered owner pursuant to the exemption afforded by Section 4(2) of said Act. No transfer or assignment of these shares by the registered owner shall be valid or effective, and the issuer shall not be required to give any effect to any transfer or attempted transfer of these shares, including without limitation, a transfer by operation of law (a) the issuer shall have received an opinion of its counsel that the shares may be transferred without requirement without of registration under said Act, or (b) there shall have been delivered to the issuer a 'no-action' letter from the staff of the Securities and Exchange Commission, or (c) the shares are registered under said Act."

5. Non-Transferability. Neither the option hereby granted nor any rights thereunder or under this Agreement may be assigned, transferred or in any

manner encumbered except by will or the laws of decent and distribution, and any attempted assignment, transfer, mortgage, pledge or encumbrance except as herein authorized, shall be void and of no effect. The option may be exercised during Optionee's lifetime only by him.

6. Termination of Employment. In the event of the termination of Optionee other than by death, the option granted may be exercised at the times and to the extent provided in paragraph 9 of the plan.

7. Death of Optionee. In the event of the death of Optionee during the term of this Agreement and while he is employed by the Company (or a subsidiary), or within three (3) months after the termination of his employment (or one(1) year in the case of the termination of employment of an Optionee under his last will, or by his personal representatives or distributees, at any time within a period of one (1) year after his death, but not after ten (10) years from the date hereof, and only if and to the extent that he was entitled to exercise the option at the date of his death.

8. Shares Issued on Exercise of Option. It is the intention of he Company that on any exercise of this option it will transfer to Optionee shares or its authorized but unissued stock or transfer Treasury shares, or utilize any combination of Treasury shares and authorized but unissued shares, to satisfy its obligations to deliver shares on any exercise hereof. Notwithstanding the foregoing, so long as the Deposit and Trust Agreement referred to in Paragraph 2 of the Plan remains in effect, Optionee will be issued Common Stock Trust Receipts upon exercise of this option in lieu of shares of Common Stock in accordance with the terms of said Agreement.

9. Committee Administration. This option has been granted pursuant to a determination made by the Committee, and such Committee or any successor or substitute committee authorized by the Board of Directors itself, subject to the express terms of this option, shall have plenary authority to interpret any provision of this option and to make any determination necessary or advisable for the administration of this option and the exercise of the rights herein granted, and may waive or amend any provisions hereof in any manner not adversely affecting the rights granted to Optionee by the express terms hereof.

IN WITNESS WHEREOF, the Company has caused this Agreement to be executed on its behalf by its Vice President and to be attested by its Secretary under the seal of the Company, pursuant to due authorization, and Optionee has signed this Agreement to evidence his acceptance of the option herein granted and of he terms hereof, all as of the date hereof.

ABC CORPORATION

By _____

     Vice President

ATTEST:

_____

     Secretary

_____

     Optionee

Sample of Option Agreement with Resale Provisions

New Tech Company Notice of Grant of Stock Option

Notice is hereby given of the following option grant (the "Option") to purchase shares of the Common Stock of New Tech Company (the "Corporation"):

Optionee: _____

Grant Date: _____

Vesting Commencement Date:_____

Exercise Price: $_____per share

Number of Option Shares: _____ shares

Expiration Date: _____

Type of Option: _____Incentive Stock Option

               _____Non-Statutory Stock Option

Date Exercisable: Immediately Exercisable

Vesting Schedule: The Option Shares shall be unvested and subject to repurchase by the Corporation at the Exercise Price paid per share. Optionee shall acquire a vested interest in, and the Corporation's repurchase right shall accordingly lapse with respect to, (i) sixteen percent (16%) of the Option Shares upon Optionee's completion of one (1) year of Service measured from the Vesting Commencement Date and (ii) the balance of the Option Shares in six (6) equal successive installments upon Optionee's completion of each six (6)-month period of Service over such three (3)-year period measured from and after the first anniversary of the Vesting Commencement Date. In no event shall any additional Option Shares vest after Optionee's cessation of Service.

Optionee understands and agrees that the Option is granted subject to and in accordance with the terms of the New Tech Company 1995 Stock Option/Stock Issuance Plan (the "Plan"). Optionee further agrees to be bound by the terms of the Plan and the terms of the Option as set forth in the Stock Option Agreement attached hereto as Exhibit A. Optionee understands that any Option Shares purchased under the Option will be subject to the terms set forth in the Stock Purchase Agreement attached hereto as Exhibit B.

Optionee hereby acknowledges receipt of a copy of the Plan in the form attached hereto as Exhibit C.

REPURCHASE RIGHTS. OPTIONEE HEREBY AGREES THAT ALL OPTION SHARES ACQUIRED UPON THE EXERCISE OF THE OPTION SHALL BE SUBJECT TO CERTAIN REPURCHASE RIGHTS AND RIGHTS OF FIRST REFUSAL EXERCISABLE BY THE CORPORATION AND ITS ASSIGNS. THE TERMS OF SUCH RIGHTS ARE SPECIFIED IN THE ATTACHED STOCK PURCHASE AGREEMENT.

No Employment or Service Contract. Nothing in this Notice or in the attached Stock Option Agreement or Plan shall confer upon Optionee any right to continue in Service for any period of specific duration or interfere with or otherwise restrict in any way the rights of the Corporation (or any Parent or Subsidiary employing or retaining Optionee) or of Optionee, which rights are hereby expressly reserved by each, to terminate Optionee's Service at any time for any reason, with or without cause.

Definitions. All capitalized terms in this Notice shall have the meaning assigned to them in this Notice or in the attached Stock Option Agreement.

_____, 199____ Date

NEW TECH COMPANY

By:_____

Title:_____

_____

OPTIONEE

Address:_____

_____

Section 83(b) Election Statement

The undersigned taxpayer hereby elects under IRC Section 83(b) as follows:

Taxpayer name:_____

Address: _____

_____

Social Security Number:_____

Description of property with respect to which the election is made.

_____

_____

The date on which the property was transferred: _____

Taxable year with respect to which the election is made: _____

Nature of the restrictions to which the property is subject:

_____

_____

Fair market value _____

Amount (if any) paid
for the property _____

Excess of fair market value
over the amount paid   _____

I have provided copies of this statement as required under the regulations for Section 83.

Dated this the____day of_____, 20__.

Signed_____

      Signature of Employee

Form **6251**	Alternative Minimum Tax—Individuals	OMB No. 1545-0227
	See separate instructions.	19**99**
Department of the Treasury Internal Revenue Service (99)	Attach to Form 1040 or Form 1040NR.	Attachment Sequence No. 32
Name(s) shown on Form 1040		Your social security number

Part I   Adjustments and Preferences

1	If you itemized deductions on Schedule A (Form 1040), go to line 2. Otherwise, enter your standard deduction from Form 1040, line 36, here and go to line 6	1	
2	Medical and dental. Enter the smaller of Schedule A (Form 1040), line 4 or 2½% of Form 1040, line 34	2	
3	Taxes. Enter the amount from Schedule A (Form 1040), line 9	3	
4	Certain interest on a home mortgage not used to buy, build, or improve your home	4	
5	Miscellaneous itemized deductions. Enter the amount from Schedule A (Form 1040), line 26	5	
6	Refund of taxes. Enter any tax refund from Form 1040, line 10 or line 21	6 ( )	
7	Investment interest. Enter difference between regular tax and AMT deduction	7	
8	Post-1986 depreciation. Enter difference between regular tax and AMT depreciation	8	
9	Adjusted gain or loss. Enter difference between AMT and regular tax gain or loss	9	
10	Incentive stock options. Enter excess of AMT income over regular tax income	10	
11	Passive activities. Enter difference between AMT and regular tax income or loss	11	
12	Beneficiaries of estates and trusts. Enter the amount from Schedule K-1 (Form 1041), line 9	12	
13	Tax-exempt interest from private activity bonds issued after 8/7/86	13	
14	Other. Enter the amount, if any, for each item below and enter the total on line 14.		

a	Circulation expenditures		h	Loss limitations
b	Depletion		i	Mining costs
c	Depreciation (pre-1987)		j	Patron's adjustment
d	Installment sales		k	Pollution control facilities
e	Intangible drilling costs		l	Research and experimental
f	Large partnerships		m	Section 1202 exclusion
g	Long-term contracts		n	Tax shelter farm activities
			o	Related adjustments

		14	
15	Total Adjustments and Preferences. Combine lines 1 through 14	15	

Part II   Alternative Minimum Taxable Income

16	Enter the amount from Form 1040, line 37. If less than zero, enter as a (loss)	16	
17	Net operating loss deduction, if any, from Form 1040, line 21. Enter as a positive amount	17	
18	If Form 1040, line 34, is over $126,600 (over $63,300 if married filing separately) and you itemized deductions enter the amount, if any, from line 9 of the worksheet for Schedule A (Form 1040), line 28	18 ( )	
19	Combine lines 15 through 18	19	
20	Alternative tax net operating loss deduction. See page 6 of the instructions	20	
21	Alternative Minimum Taxable Income. Subtract line 20 from line 19. (If married filing separately and line 21 is more than $165,000, see page 7 of the instructions.)	21	

Part III   Exemption Amount and Alternative Minimum Tax

22	Exemption Amount. (If this form is for a child under age 14, see page 7 of the instructions.)		

IF your filing status is . . .	AND line 21 is not over . . .	THEN enter on line 22 . . .	
Single or head of household	$112,500	$33,750	
Married filing jointly or qualifying widow(er)	150,000	45,000	22
Married filing separately	75,000	22,500	

	If line 21 is over the amounts shown above for your filing status, see page 7 of the instructions.		
23	Subtract line 22 from line 21. If zero or less, enter -0- here and on lines 26 and 28	23	
24	If you reported capital gain distributions directly on Form 1040, line 13, or you completed Schedule D (Form 1040) and have an amount on line 25 or line 27 (or would have had an amount on either line if you had completed Part IV) (as refigured for the AMT, if necessary) go to Part IV of Form 6251 to figure line 24. All others: If line 23 is $175,000 or less ($87,500 or less if married filing separately) multiply line 23 by 26% (.26). Otherwise, multiply line 23 by 28% (.28) and subtract $3,500 ($1,750 if married filing separately) from the result	24	
25	Alternative minimum tax foreign tax credit. See page 7 of the instructions	25	
26	Tentative minimum tax. Subtract line 25 from line 24	26	
27	Enter your tax from Form 1040, line 40 (minus any tax from Form 4972 and any foreign tax credit from Form 1040, line 46)	27	
28	Alternative Minimum Tax. Subtract line 27 from line 26. If zero or less, enter -0-. Enter here and on Form 1040, line 51	28	

For Paperwork Reduction Act Notice, see page 8 of the instructions.	Cat. No. 13600G	Form **6251** (1999)

Form 6251 (1999)   Page 2

Part IV   Line 24 Computation Using Maximum Capital Gains Rates

Caution: If you **did not** complete Part IV of Schedule D (Form 1040), see page 8 of the instructions before you complete this part.

29	Enter the amount from Form 6251, line 23	29
30	Enter the amount from Schedule D (Form 1040), line 27 (as refigured for the AMT, if necessary) See page 8 of the instructions ... 30	
31	Enter the amount from Schedule D (Form 1040), line 25 (as refigured for the AMT, if necessary) See page 8 of the instructions ... 31	
32	Add lines 30 and 31 ... 32	
33	Enter the amount from Schedule D (Form 1040), line 22 (as refigured for the AMT, if necessary) See page 8 of the instructions ... 33	
34	Enter the smaller of line 32 or line 33	34
35	Subtract line 34 from line 29. If zero or less, enter -0-	35
36	If line 35 is $175,000 or less ($87,500 or less if married filing separately) multiply line 35 by 26% (.26). Otherwise, multiply line 35 by 28% (.28) and subtract $3,500 ($1,750 if married filing separately) from the result	36
37	Enter the amount from Schedule D (Form 1040), line 36 (as figured for the regular tax). See page 8 of the instructions ... 37	
38	Enter the smallest of line 29, line 30, or line 37 ... 38	
39	Multiply line 38 by 10% (.10)	39
40	Enter the smaller of line 29 or line 30 ... 40	
41	Enter the amount from line 38 ... 41	
42	Subtract line 41 from line 40 ... 42	
43	Multiply line 42 by 20% (.20)	43
	Note: If line 31 is zero or blank, go to line 48.	
44	Enter the amount from line 29 ... 44	
45	Add lines 35, 38, and 42 ... 45	
46	Subtract line 45 from line 44 ... 46	
47	Multiply line 46 by 25% (.25)	47
48	Add lines 36, 39, 43, and 47	48
49	If line 29 is $175,000 or less ($87,500 or less if married filing separately) multiply line 29 by 26% (.26). Otherwise, multiply line 29 by 28% (.28) and subtract $3,500 ($1,750 if married filing separately) from the result	49
50	Enter the smaller of line 48 or line 49 here and on line 24	50

Form **6251** (1999)

Made in the USA